CONNECTING THE DOTS

How God's Sovereignty Affects You and Me

Arthur Enns

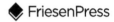 FriesenPress

Suite 300 - 990 Fort St
Victoria, BC, V8V 3K2
Canada

www.friesenpress.com

Book ordering and contact information: www.arthurenns.com

ISBN
978-1-03-910004-6 (Hardcover)
978-1-03-910003-9 (Paperback)
978-1-03-910005-3 (eBook)

Religion, Christian Life, Spiritual Growth

Distributed to the trade by The Ingram Book Company

Arthur Enns has the spiritual writer's gift of expressing simply and vividly the often difficult and abstract issues of theology. Perhaps no other theme is so vital to be heard afresh in our day as that of the sovereignty of God. Arthur's clear thinking, lucid prose, and personal stories winsomely draw the reader's mind and heart into the realm of our glorious King.

—Mike Mason, author of *The Mystery of Marriage* and *Champagne for the Soul*

Connecting the Dots tackles some pretty complex issues in a beautifully simple, but not simplistic, way. If we believe that God is in charge of our lives and all things in this world, how do we reconcile that with difficulty in our lives, in sometimes having to live with circumstances that would definitely be "second choice" for us? How do we live with the tension of prayers not being answered the way we would like them answered, or with things not happening in the timing we expect?

Arthur, a friend I have known for several decades, demonstrates a deep faith which shines through some painful experiences. I highly commend this book, which is practical, faith-filled, and wonderfully theological in a down-to-earth way.

—Steve Thomas, International Team Leader, *Salt & Light* family of churches

Connecting the Dots is a thought-provoking and enjoyable read. Arthur succeeds in bringing home the truth of God's sovereignty in a real and personal way that draws the reader into a place of wonder and awe. For anyone grappling with life's tough questions as to why God would allow us to go through difficult trials, this book will benefit you.

Through down-to-earth stories, Arthur enables us to see that God remains close to each one of us, even in times of weakness and mistakes. As we discover in the pages of this important book, God actually chooses to involve himself with us, and our imperfections simply qualify us for his transforming work.

You'll want to take your time as you read this personal journey of understanding God's workings in our lives. Definitely add this book to your library!

—Rob Parker, Founder/Director,
National House of Prayer (Canada)

In *Connecting the Dots*, Arthur Enns' life experiences—as family man, business executive, community builder, pastor, and friend—are skillfully linked with eternal truth, bringing my blurred understanding of the sovereignty of God into sharp focus, and applying that clarity to areas of life I had not previously considered.

Significant loss touches each of us. As the death of Arthur's wife propelled his search for answers, this book allowed me to revisit my own losses, reflecting on them in light of a sovereign God who was actively participating in every detail of each day, and reminding me that while the storm rages, I have a strong and sure anchor!

I consider the time spent reading this book a valuable investment in my spiritual well-being.

—Phyllis I. Simon, *BC Notary Public*

I count Arthur Enns as a long-standing friend who speaks truth tempered with compassion. My first encounter with him was a few decades ago when I was attending Bible School and he was a visiting lecturer. The topic he chose for the week was "Honor"—recognizing the value and worth in each person because of the image of God.

In this, his first book, Arthur takes honoring to both its source and final conclusion: honoring God. It's "connecting the dots" to see how God's overarching and under-girding *Being* provides the context for our own being and understanding.

Through little phrases, short sentences, and thoughts forged by the joys and troubles of life, all carefully crafted to honor both God and the reader, the dots come together to form a recognizable picture. Well done, my friend!

—Charlie Whitley, Pastor, *Vernon Christian Fellowship*

In loving memory of
Margarete (Martens) Enns

Contents

Preface   xv

Introduction   1

Section One *Sovereignty Gets Personal*   9

> **Chapter 1**
> A Hawaiian Traffic Jam
> *Sovereignty and Grace (Part 1)*   11

> **Chapter 2**
> Lone Rider No More
> *Sovereignty and Grace (Part 2)*   15

> **Chapter 3**
> A Perfect Mess
> *Sovereignty and Character Flaws (Part 1)*   19

> **Chapter 4**
> An Unstable Rock
> *Sovereignty and Character Flaws (Part 2)*   23

> **Chapter 5**
> Terror, Trash-Talk, or Trust?
> *Sovereignty and Our Strengths*   27

> **Chapter 6**
> To Judge or Not to Judge?
> *Sovereignty and Judging (Part 1)*   31

> **Chapter 7**
> Judge, Jury, and Executioner
> *Sovereignty and Judging (Part 2)*   35

Chapter 8
My Best Executive Decision *Sovereignty and Direction (Part 1)* 39

Chapter 9
Beetles and Betelgeuse
Sovereignty and Direction (Part 2) 43

Chapter 10
Carpe Diem!
Sovereignty and Ambition 47

Chapter 11
Impossible Forgetfulness
Sovereignty and Forgiveness (Part 1) 51

Chapter 12
The Inexcusable
Sovereignty and Forgiveness (Part 2) 55

Chapter 13
Choosing Our Fears
Sovereignty and Fear (Part 1) 59

Chapter 14
Dullards in the Storm
Sovereignty and Fear (Part 2) 63

Chapter 15
Seal of Approval
Sovereignty and Humility 67

Chapter 16
Recalculating
Sovereignty and Our Mistakes 71

Chapter 17
Bright Hope for Tomorrow
Sovereignty and My Future 75

Chapter 18
Personal Preference
Sovereignty and God's Messengers   *79*

Chapter 19
The Cost of Relationship
What a Sovereign God Values Most   *83*

Chapter 20
Reality Therapy
Sovereignty and Subjectivity   *87*

Chapter 21
What Cancer Cannot Steal
God's Sovereignty as a Win-Win   *91*

Chapter 22
The Heart Has Its Reasons
Sovereign Surprises   *95*

Section Two *Sovereignty Touches Everything*   **99**

Introduction to Section 2 *If God Were Not Sovereign…*   **101**

Chapter 23
No Limits
Sovereignty and Infinity   *107*

Chapter 24
A Fine-Tuned You
Sovereignty and DNA   *111*

Chapter 25
Coincidence, Control, or Chance?
Sovereignty and Probability (Part 1)   *115*

Chapter 26
Luck of the Draw
Sovereignty and Probability (Part 2)   *119*

Chapter 27
A One-Owner World
Sovereignty and Ownership (Part 1) 123

Chapter 28
All Creatures Great and Small
Sovereignty and Ownership (Part 2) 127

Chapter 29
My Choice or God's Will?
Sovereignty, Free Will, and Election 131

Chapter 30
Smite Makes Right?
Sovereignty, Justice, and Judgment (Part 1) 135

Chapter 31
Justice Delayed
Sovereignty, Justice, and Judgment (Part 2) 139

Chapter 32
Running with Bulls and Angels
God's Sovereignty and Our Safety 143

Chapter 33
The Mysteries of Misery
Sovereignty, Pain, and Suffering (Part 1) 147

Chapter 34
Is There Meaning in Tragedy?
Sovereignty, Pain, and Suffering (Part 2) 151

Chapter 35
On Hold with Heaven
God's Sovereign Timing 155

Chapter 36
A Poor Substitute
Sovereignty and Temptation 159

Chapter 37
Heavenly Parties
Sovereignty and God's Emotions (Part 1)   *163*

Chapter 38
From Bliss to Blues
Sovereignty and God's Emotions (Part 2)   *167*

Chapter 39
The Right to Look
Sovereignty and Sex   *171*

Chapter 40
Image of God
Sovereignty and Racism   *175*

Chapter 41
Just Between You and God
Sovereignty, Relationships, and Time   *179*

Chapter 42
CEO of Heaven and Earth
The Sovereignty of the Son   *183*

Chapter 43
What If…?
The Sovereign Foreknowledge of God (Part 1)   *187*

Chapter 44
Blissfully Unaware
The Sovereign Foreknowledge of God (Part 2)   *191*

Appendix: What About the Bible?   195

Selected Bibliography   203

Acknowledgments   205

About the Author   207

Preface

This was meant to be a more theoretical book—a tidy collection of ideas and insights gained from years of study and experience. But a few life-changing events intervened.

One of those was the death of my wife, which impacted both my faith journey and my awareness of things buried deep within my mind and emotions.

I knew there was a choice to be made. I could maintain my usual preference for privacy, or I could become more open and honest with God, with myself, and with others.

This book is an attempt to choose the latter, the result being a combination of objective truth (for example, how God is described in the Bible) and my subjective grappling with that truth. For me, it's a process of *connecting the dots.*

In the midst of life-changing events, whether a personal tragedy or a worldwide crisis like a pandemic, the most important truth I can imagine is God's sovereignty. If God is actually in charge—if things don't just happen by chance—it changes everything. Then there's a foundation for faith, a basis for hope, and a purpose in life.

An old joke offers the advice, "Life is short; eat dessert first." Of course, that's just a way of describing life's uncertainty, of which we were reminded in 2020 as the coronavirus pandemic spread and normal life came to a standstill.

In contrast, the Bible describes God as being supreme—above it all: "He does whatever he pleases,"[1] says Job, who at the time was not at all pleased with what God was allowing, which included the loss of his wealth, his reputation, his health, and his children. *Job's complaints are valid*, we might think. But in the end, he came to understand God's sovereignty in a whole new way. Thankfully, I've not had to experience all that Job did, but my appreciation for God as the one immoveable Rock during stormy times only has increased.

In fact, the more I learn who God is, the more I'm glad that "he does whatever he pleases." Why? Because he understands it all, he's in charge of everything, he knows us, and (still surprising to me) he loves us.

I invite you to join me on a journey of discovering more about this God who does whatever he pleases. It's a quest that takes us beyond our usual way of thinking. It requires honesty and probably a dose of humility too.

Most of all, it means *connecting the dots* as we explore how God's sovereignty affects you and me.

Arthur Enns

January 2021

---

1   Job 23:13.

Introduction

I'm startled awake by the phone, and quickly reach for it in the pre-dawn darkness.

It's the charge nurse at the Palliative Care Unit, explaining in her kindly but no-nonsense way that my wife Margarete has taken a turn for the worse and that this could be her last day. I mumble an acknowledgment and tell her I'll be at the hospital shortly.

My mind is numb, trying to process what just happened.

It's not a total shock, and yet I'm thinking, *She was just in hospital for a nerve block procedure; she was still supposed to come home! How could this be the end?* As I scramble through a shower and shave, I'm so overcome by the enormity of the situation that I find myself repeating a two-word prayer: "O Jesus, O Jesus, O Jesus, O Jesus…"

The nurse's prediction turns out to be correct.

Family members and close friends join me at the hospital throughout the day, and then at nine o'clock that evening—despite months of prayer for healing on the part of family, relatives, friends, pastors, and church members—my dear wife of 39 years takes her last breath.

Like many cases of inoperable pancreatic cancer, its discovery had come as a surprise, and the timing of the diagnosis—just weeks after my retirement—instantly changed our outlook for the future. We knew that, barring a miracle, our dream of growing old together had vanished.

As it turned out, she lived another eleven months. Between medical appointments and treatments, we tried to make the most of the time we had left, planning special family times and visits with friends and colleagues.

We also moved back to the West End of Vancouver where we had spent our first year of marriage, to an apartment overlooking English Bay and Stanley Park. Margarete loved the color and culture of city life, and the seawall provided a beautiful venue for walks (eventually with me pushing her in a wheelchair) to enjoy the sea, the park, and the city lights.

The seven-mile (10-km) seawall around Stanley Park was helpful for another reason: it allowed me to take long walks on my own to think and pray and try to process what was happening.

With death staring us in the face, denial wasn't an option. Yet both of us were convinced that God was sovereign and quite capable of performing miracles. The fact that literally hundreds of people were praying for just such a miracle, some of them fasting as they prayed, was very encouraging, but we still wondered exactly what God expected of us in terms of faith.

Eventually the visiting Palliative Care nurse and social worker advised us to start the process of "final arrangements," the premise being, *hope for the best; prepare for the worst*—which seemed sensible if not exactly infused with supernatural faith. Besides (as we told ourselves), we'd need to do that at some point anyway. And so we bought a double burial plot and ordered a bronze plaque that expressed our love and faith.[1]

Then the social worker asked whether we had talked about a funeral service. We hadn't. But when we did have that somewhat awkward conversation, I was amazed to learn that Margarete had already planned most of the service—a process she'd begun months earlier. To me it was evidence of her courage and faith: courage to face death unflinchingly and faith in a God who was wise, caring, and sovereign.

The funeral turned out to be an unforgettable tribute to an unforgettably gracious and highly-esteemed woman—and to her Maker. I will never forget the outpouring of support from friends and family during that time. The genuineness and tenderness of those expressions of love brought me to tears more than once.

A month later, I set out on a personal retreat at the Oregon Coast where we had enjoyed many vacations. It was different on my own, of course, but cathartic in many ways as I spent a week reading, praying, writing, walking alongside the pounding waves from the open ocean, and expressing my raw feelings to God in a completely open and unhindered way.

In a further way of dealing with grief, I said my goodbyes to Margarete in the form of a long, heartfelt letter. (Whether the Lord shares that sort of information with people in his heavenly presence, I have no idea. But it seemed to help with my own journey.)

---

1   Several months later when the plaque arrived at the grave, I was surprised to see my own name and birth year also engraved in bronze, just awaiting those final four digits—my year of death—to be added. For anyone needing a dose of reality, that is one sure remedy!

There are always questions when you deal with life and death. For me, it wasn't a question of God's ability to intervene, or his right to do whatever he wanted with us, or his wisdom, or his goodness. Those were all core beliefs at an intellectual and theological level. But how did all that relate to the stark reality I was now facing?

I could accept that losing Margarete was somehow wrapped up in God's sovereignty, but what did that really mean? Was her death related to our limited faith in praying for healing? Was it really God's will for her to die before reaching old age? And if so, why?

The *Why?* question is hardly a new one. In the oldest book in the Bible, Job asks *Why?* more eloquently, more passionately, and with more justification than I ever could—and even he didn't get an explanation. So I'm not about to claim the discovery of answers that countless sages have pursued in vain!

Nevertheless, in reflecting on life and studying the Bible and other books over the years, I have kept notes on insights and words of wisdom that have helped me, partly for my personal benefit, but also for sharing with others.[2]

There was a time (in my youth) when I was so taken with philosophical and theological ideas that I was sure I would spend my future in a related field. As life unfolded, I found myself involved in more hands-on pursuits—in radio, in pastoral ministry, and in healthcare administration—but I've always known that someday I'd be writing.

Given my bent toward the world of ideas, I was expecting this study on God's sovereignty to be more theologically oriented. There definitely is a place for books like that, but this one turned out to be more personal and practical than I had imagined.

---

2   For those who may wonder why anyone in the 21st century should rely on an ancient holy book like the Bible, I would recommend reading the Appendix: *What About the Bible?*

Because of that, I've tried to avoid academic language. Theology has its own unique terminology in the same way that medicine, science, engineering, and law have their own vocabularies. It's not particularly helpful to throw around technical terms for readers outside those specialties.

While fancy words can help us be precise, they also can be used to obscure truth and even insulate us from responsibility, which is probably why Jesus chose to do a lot of his teaching through stories. He was more interested in getting through to the hearts of his listeners than impressing his critics.

The opposite danger, of course, is being simplistic. If I have erred in that regard, it is not due to lack of appreciation for the complexity of the subject—or any intention of writing a *Sovereignty-for-Dummies*-type of book—but rather an awareness of a deeper issue: namely, how easy it is to harbor false ideas about God and how readily my actions belie my core beliefs.

In other words, I can have all the correct doctrines about God's sovereignty in my head as "knowledge" while at the same time reacting to life's circumstances as though God didn't exist. Some call it the head-heart divide.

In the life-and-death situation involving my wife, I was brought face to face with God's sovereignty in a way that transcended theological debate. It was real. And it affected me personally.

But in principle it's no different from any other situation we face in life. Either God is involved—and making a difference—or, for all practical purposes, we're living as though we're atheists.

The format I've used is loosely borrowed from one of my favorite authors, Mike Mason, whose books of short chapters, abounding in gems of truth and grace, helped me greatly during my journey of bereavement. I appreciated that he didn't expect everyone to read from cover to cover, offering "the freedom to read any book desultorily, pausing here and there as the mood may strike."[3] Excellent advice!

Thematically, I've divided the book as follows: Section 1 includes stories from my own journey and reflections on the more personal side of God's sovereignty, while Section 2 focuses on ways in which God's sovereignty affects key dimensions of life on Earth.

And what exactly do we mean by God's sovereignty?

Insurance companies and lawyers use the term "acts of God" to describe events beyond human control such as earthquakes, volcanic eruptions, and hurricanes, while Christians talk about God being "in control of everything," but often aren't clear on what control actually means.

Dictionaries offer synonyms like *ultimate authority, preeminence, dominion,* and *supreme and unrestricted power.*

One of the writers of the Psalms puts it into simple poetic form:

> The Lord does whatever pleases him,
> > in the heavens and on the earth,
> > in the seas and all their depths.[4]

It all boils down to this: God's sovereignty means he *knows everything, and he can do anything.*

We're talking about total knowledge combined with absolute power. But that begs the question, *If that is true, how is it a good thing?*

If we're dealing with someone who is very powerful but also an ogre, we're in trouble. And it's not much better if the "good guy" in a given situation is powerless. The only way God's sovereignty is good news is if God is both all-powerful and all-good.

---

3   Mike Mason, *The Gospel According to Job*, rev. ed. (1994; repr., Wheaton, Ill: Crossway, 2002), *xiii.*

4   Psalm 135:6.

A hymn written two centuries ago and still sung today[5] describes this God as "merciful and mighty"—a combination that makes all the difference for you and me. That's the God whose sovereignty we'll be exploring in this book.

He's already taken the first steps to connect with us. Our part is to open our eyes and connect the dots.

---

5   "Holy, Holy, Holy! Lord God Almighty," written by Reginald Heber in 1826.

Section One

Sovereignty Gets Personal

Chapter 1

A Hawaiian Traffic Jam
Sovereignty and Grace (Part 1)

Being administratively oriented, I'm prepared for most eventualities. That includes carrying insurance—medical, disability, fire, flood, liability, theft, collision, etc.—because you never know what might happen.

But one type of insurance I could never bring myself to buy was life insurance on my wife. Maybe it was a kind of denial, but somewhere in the recesses of my soul was the idea that her dying (before she was old) would be such an unimaginable tragedy that collecting life insurance would be pointless. In the wake of such a loss I couldn't see anything mattering very much, least of all money.

But then the unimaginable happened.

After dealing with back pain and stomach troubles for many months, Margarete received a phone call from our doctor one Friday evening saying that her X-rays were indicating pancreatic cancer, a diagnosis that was soon confirmed as inoperable and terminal.

We didn't sleep much that night because of the shock of the news, but there was also a sense of peace and God's care for us. Margarete spent time that evening playing the piano and singing to the Lord. And I went out the next day to a park by the Fraser River to think and pray and try to process what we had heard.

The strange thing was the sense of peace we felt right from the start of that journey. It must have been the "peace that passes understanding" the Bible talks about[1] because it really was unexplainable, especially in light of my long-standing refusal to consider her death in anything but tragic terms.

That peace was a timely expression of God's grace, given exactly when we needed it. Later, God's grace also came in the form of helpful insights from a real-life parable.

After several rounds of chemotherapy that had brought her symptoms under better control, we decided to risk one last trip to Hawaii. I learned that travel medical insurance is not available for those with terminal illness, so I took along all my credit cards "just in case."

The trip went well, all things considered. I even rented a convertible one day for a driving tour around the island, which led to an unforgettable lesson.

We arrived at a T-junction where a long line of cars was coming from the right, stopping, then going through the three-way intersection. Given my aversion to long lines, I decided to turn right, happily zipping past all the cars waiting to turn left.

What I didn't realize was that my right turn was taking me on a closed loop that just brought me back to where all the cars were lined up—except now it meant waiting over an hour in traffic!

The next day I had a sense that God was using this traffic scenario as an illustration. I was facing a situation like that intersection and had a choice to make in dealing with my wife's terminal illness. I could choose to feel the pain but also experience God's grace. Or I

---

1   Philippians 4:7.

could respond by choosing what seemed an easier path, represented by reactions like escapism, stoicism, and anger.

Escapism would be trying to avoid thinking about the situation by means of various diversions. Stoicism would involve pretending everything was fine, and stuffing my feelings of grief and loss. Anger would be dwelling on how unfair it was for this to happen to Margarete and how it robbed us of our dream of growing old together.

What I felt God was saying to me was this: Just as taking the wrong turn did not eliminate the traffic jam but just delayed and compounded it, a wrong choice in responding to my wife's illness would not deal with the pain either, but just postpone it and ultimately make it worse.

That insight was like gold to me. In the months that followed, it helped me choose to accept the pain, but also experience God's peace, comfort, and joy in the process.

There was a further application, as I note from my journal a few weeks later:

> *I had assumed that the lesson was just referring to the pain of dealing with Margarete's condition and the prospect of bereavement. I now see that it refers to any and all things that cause pain, including:*
>
> - *Frustrating circumstances*
> - *Failure (in any area)*
> - *Confusion about God's plan or direction*
> - *Unresolved issues—especially as they accumulate*
> - *Undone tasks*
> - *Injustice (including what I see on the news)*
>
> *I have not previously associated these things with "pain," but the fact is: I do find them to be troubling—and thus painful— to my soul. Therefore I need to learn to take all these things to*

the Lord and seek his comfort, his answer, his grace, his provision—rather than trying to dull the pain by my own efforts via escapism, ignoring it (stoicism), or responding with anger.

I wish I could say I've responded the right way ever since, but that wouldn't be true. However, there's been progress.

In retrospect, I believe my refusal to buy life insurance on my wife indicated a deep-seated fear of losing her. I couldn't begin to imagine the sense of devastation I would experience if that ever happened, and so I avoided any thoughts in that direction.

But when the time came, God was there. And instead of devastation, there was amazing grace. Only a sovereign God could do that.

Chapter 2

Lone Rider No More
Sovereignty and Grace (Part 2)

Despite an active social life from my earliest years, I've always enjoyed solitude.[1]

As a 20-year-old, sporting the longish hair and beard common to the hippy era, I happily embarked on a solitary motorcycle trip from British Columbia to southern California and back, exploring new cities, the Redwoods, and the spectacular Pacific coastline.[2]

But I've also discovered that solitude can be overrated. After my wife passed away, the quietness in my Vancouver apartment seemed overwhelming at times, and I soon got in the habit of turning on the TV news to ease the silence during dinner.

While we may experience a certain grace when we're alone— away from the noise and busyness of life and interactions with

---

1   In fact, I'm writing this chapter while staying alone at a remote cabin in the Monashee Mountains of British Columbia.

2   One of my goals was to have enough time to figure out life's quandaries, but that never quite happened!

family members and friends—there is also much grace that comes via people.

That certainly was my experience during my wife's battle with cancer, her passing, and the subsequent journey of bereavement. In fact, I often wondered how others in my situation could handle these challenges all on their own—without the Lord, but also without the support of loving family members, loyal friends, caring colleagues, or committed church members. It wasn't a stretch to imagine myself turning to alcohol or drugs in the absence of those relationships.

It was in that environment of care and support that I sent out the following email when my wife died:

Hi family and friends:

>*You may have already heard, but I'm sending this update to ensure all of you are aware of what has happened. Margarete passed away peacefully at nine o'clock last night at St. Paul's Hospital, surrounded by family, friends, and pastors who were there throughout the day.*
>
>*While Margarete wasn't able to respond at that point, the nurses felt that she could still hear and comprehend, so we communicated our love (and the love of those who couldn't be there), sang songs, prayed, listened to music, and just held her hand. It was a day I will never forget, filled with many different emotions: the grief of imminent loss, but also the hope of knowing that she was going to a place of incredible joy and peace.*
>
>*Thank you again for your prayers on our behalf. Even though God doesn't always answer in the way we would choose, he is always loving, gracious, and wise in his care for us.*
>
>*We will still be having Thanksgiving together as a family, except that Margarete will be elsewhere, enjoying a feast that we couldn't even imagine. I already miss her very much, and I know that's true for everyone who got to know her.*

Even now as I read those words—years after the fact—I feel the pang of emotion that accompanied her loss. There's no getting around the fact that people are irreplaceable. The unique personality given to each of us by our Creator can never be duplicated.

That's the real and ongoing pain of death. And yet the Bible tells us, "Death has been swallowed up in victory."[3] What does that mean?

It means, among other things, that Jesus's resurrection guarantees our own resurrection, and so death is not a permanent separation for those in Christ. There's an unavoidable sense of loss, but it's a separation with the sure hope of reunion (albeit not in a marriage-type relationship, as Jesus made clear in his teaching about our future state).[4]

A few weeks after Margarete's passing, I found it helpful to get away on my own to process what had happened. I took long walks beside the ocean, read a book about another man's journey of bereavement, and freely expressed to the Lord my own grief, my questions, my hopes, my faith, everything.

But in the end, it was God's grace through *people* that helped me rebuild after a life-altering event—that made a healthy renewal possible.

Besides anything else, their sustained prayers gave me a sense that not only was everything possible being done medically, but also spiritually, and that even if my own faith were deficient in some way, God was also hearing the prayers of hundreds of others.[5]

In the process, I also learned that God's grace through people is not a one-way street. It involves intentional steps by both parties—deliberate choices to maintain, renew, and strengthen relationships.

---

3   1 Corinthians 15:54.

4   Matthew 22:30.

5   Of course, answers to prayer are not dependent on the number of people praying, but it's incredibly encouraging when there is that level of support.

God, in his sovereignty, chooses to dispense some of his grace to us directly; other grace he gives indirectly—through others.

Which is what the apostle Peter seemed to have in mind when he gave this word of counsel:

> Each of you should use whatever gift you have received to serve others, as faithful stewards of God's grace in its various forms.[6]

I'm sure I'll always appreciate my alone times, but I can't thank God enough for the blessing of his people.

---

6   1 Peter 4:10.

Chapter 3

A Perfect Mess
Sovereignty and Character Flaws (Part 1)

The stories in the Bible have at least one thing in common with daytime television talk shows: they include confessions about people's failures and weaknesses—although not for the same reasons.

TV hosts try to get their guests to reveal their darkest secrets because it spices up the interview and increases ratings. When Bible writers do a tell-all about their subject, it's meant to teach a lesson. But it's also because God wants us to know that he works with "the good, the bad, and the ugly," and that our weaknesses don't overrule his sovereignty.

I was reminded of that recently while reading a historical novel based on the life of King David.[1] As with other heroes of the faith in Scripture, David's character flaws and failures are on full display. But they don't *define* him, nor do they ultimately cancel the

---

1   Mark Buchanan, *David: Rise* (M.A. Buchanan, Inc., 2020). This is Book One of *The David Trilogy*, and part of Buchanan's superb bibliography.

purposes of God in his life—which is good news for the rest of us flawed creatures.

Human weaknesses often loom large, especially in the lives of those who act impulsively or say whatever they're thinking. But I'm reminded of something the apostle Paul wrote: "The sins of some are obvious, reaching the place of judgment ahead of them; the sins of others trail behind them."[2]

The point is: whether our weaknesses are obvious or well-hidden, we all struggle with them, and—unless we're insulated from reality due to fame, drugs, or denial—we become more aware of them the older we get.

There are times when life seems very messy. I'm looking at a journal entry from a few years ago when I wrote:

> *Everywhere I look, I see messiness and complication. There's the political morass in the UK and the USA; troubles in the church and family; messy piles of paper in my office and seemingly endless lists of undone things; and my lack of personal discipline—e.g., too little exercise, too much snacking, and spending too much time on news and entertainment.*[3]

To those of us with perfectionistic tendencies, messiness can be unsettling or even tormenting. One Scripture that applies to life's inadequacies is a short couplet from the longest Psalm in the Bible:

To all perfection I see a limit,

but your commands are boundless.[4]

For some reason, I find it helpful to be reminded that every part of life on earth is incomplete, imperfect—no exception.

---

2   1 Timothy 5:24.

3   One might assume that was an entry from the pandemic lockdown of 2020, but alas, no such excuse; it was well before that.

4   Psalm 119:96.

Back in my journal entry on this subject, I found further encouragement:

> *I believe God showed me that he had worked with messiness from the beginning of creation, and that it really wasn't a problem to him. I started to see my perfectionism as a ploy of the enemy to distract me from simple faith, using my reaction to messes as a way of fomenting discouragement and escapism. I was also reminded of the fact that God is HUGE, and that my problems and failures—and this world's problems and failures—pale into insignificance in the light of his grace and power.*

So the real issue is our focus: Are we looking at ourselves, or are we looking to God?

Author Dudley Hall explains that our problems really began a long time ago with the first humans choosing independence from God and then hiding from him in fear and shame:

> Since that time, natural human beings have been living self-consciously. Some are conscious of how well they are doing; others are conscious of how poorly they are doing, but all are enamored of self. And just about everybody is looking for some place to hide.
>
> All of fallen humanity has a consciousness of being incomplete and flawed. This is the result of original sin in the human race. We are imperfect in the presence of God who is absolutely perfect. So we stand vulnerable to exposure but terribly afraid.[5]

But there's good news—as the writer goes on to say:

---

5   Dudley Hall, *Grace Works* (Euless, Texas: Kerygma Ventures, 2013), 190.

So what answer did God, in his grace, give to our needy human predicament? Significantly, it didn't involve calling us to endless self-examination nor browbeating us with the law. His answer to our pitiful plight was to send his Son. Jesus came to live under the law; to defeat our enemies of sin, Satan, and death through the cross; and to be raised again so that our eyes could be taken off ourselves and put on Jesus.

In other words, the only cure for self-consciousness and sin-consciousness is God-consciousness.[6]

When the apostle Paul pleaded with the Lord to take away a long-standing personal problem, he got an unexpected answer:

> But he said to me, "My grace is sufficient for you, for my power is made perfect in weakness." Therefore I will boast all the more gladly about my weaknesses, so that Christ's power may rest on me... For when I am weak, then I am strong.[7]

Weakness counting as strength; messiness encompassed by perfection. It's true, it's liberating, and it's all part of the amazing sovereignty of God.

---

6   Hall, 302.

7   2 Corinthians 12:9-10.

Chapter 4

An Unstable Rock
Sovereignty and Character Flaws (Part 2)

One of the highlights of our Israel tour in 2019 was seeing the ruins of a synagogue in Capernaum and, nearby, the rock foundations of what many academics agree was Simon Peter's house.[1]

Buildings in Israel have always used stone as a primary building material. I couldn't help but notice from the windows of our tour bus how plentiful stones are in Israel, and my thoughts went in a darker direction as I realized how easy it would have been to execute people by stoning (in ancient times) or to engage in a stone-throwing *intifada* (in modern times).

As it turns out, stone was also the foundation of the name Jesus gave to a fisherman who was to become his leading disciple:

---

1   https://www.biblicalarchaeology.org/daily/
biblical-sites-places/biblical-archaeology-sites/
the-house-of-peter-the-home-of-jesus-in-capernaum/.

Jesus looked at him and said, "You are Simon son of John. You will be called Cephas" (which, when translated, is Peter).[2]

In both Aramaic and Greek, the new name means "rock," which sounds very solid and foundational. Except that it doesn't quite fit.

For all his strengths, Peter tends to say whatever enters his mind, he acts impulsively, he's given to boasting, and he wavers under pressure. All very human traits, but not what you'd look for in a rock-solid leader.

Let's look at the Biblical record:

- On the one hand, Peter is commended for his declaration of who Jesus is ("You are the Messiah"), but then he's sharply rebuked ("Get behind me, Satan!") when he tries to deter Jesus from the way of the cross.[3]

- During the transfiguration of Jesus, one of the most awe-inspiring scenes recorded in Scripture, Peter starts jabbering about building shelters for Jesus, Moses, and Elijah. The Gospel writer Luke charitably adds the note, "He did not know what he was saying." At which point God interrupts Peter's verbal barrage by refocusing attention on Jesus: "This is my Son, whom I have chosen; listen to him."[4]

- The Gospels record several occasions when the disciples argued about which of them was the greatest. No one is named, but it's impossible to imagine Peter abstaining from those debates!

- When Jesus told the disciples at the Last Supper that they would all fall away, Peter declared, "Even if all

---

2   John 1:42.

3   Matthew 16:16-23.

4   Luke 9:28-35.

fall away on account of you, I never will." Then, after being told that he would disown Jesus three times that very night, Peter insists, "Even if I have to die with you, I will never disown you." But, of course, he did— in the process repeating a few choice swearwords from his fisherman days.[5]

- Even after Peter's transformation into the bold, Spirit-filled leader we read about in the Book of Acts, it's not the end of his lapses. Paul writes how he had to publicly rebuke Peter at Antioch for the way he was treating the Gentile Christians there.[6]

To be honest, I feel a bit churlish in highlighting Peter's faults. None of us would appreciate having our failings exposed to the world. But I'm assuming that God wouldn't have recorded these things in Scripture if he didn't want us to learn from them.

And what do we learn?

That even the top leaders in the Bible are flawed? *Yes.*

That spending time with Jesus doesn't result in instant character change? *Regrettably true.*

That even being Spirit-filled and performing major miracles doesn't guarantee someone is right on a particular subject? *Exactly.*

But there's more than that.

Imagine if Peter somehow could be featured on the long-running television game show *To Tell the Truth,* and the announcer said, "Will the real Simon Peter please stand up?"

Would it be the sincere but blustering Peter from his early days as a disciple? Or the apostle in the early church who was famous for his

---

5   Matthew 26:31-35, 69-75.

6   Galatians 2:11-14. Peter evidently accepted this correction as there is no record of a split. In fact, years later Peter calls Paul "our dear brother," and refers to his letters as Scriptures (2 Peter 3:15-16).

powerful messages and miracles, and who was on track *most* of the time? Or the older, gracious yet prophetic leader who wrote letters that became part of Scripture?

The enemy of our souls would say, "The real Peter is a vacillating braggart with an unreliable track record."

But Jesus would say, "This impetuous man with a flawed character is someone I will work on until he becomes the man I intend him to be. In fact, I'm changing his name to *Rock*. *That's* the real Peter."

It takes a sovereign God to bring about that kind of transformation. Nothing less will do.

No matter what the enemy whispers in our ear, our character flaws are never greater than God's sovereignty. As a result, none of us is hopeless or incorrigible.

As the great apostle Peter wrote in his later years:

> Humble yourselves, therefore, under God's mighty hand, that he may lift you up in due time. Cast all your anxiety on him because he cares for you.
> And the God of all grace, who called you to his eternal glory in Christ, after you have suffered a little while, will himself restore you and make you strong, firm and steadfast.[7]

In God, the unstable rock transforms—gradually—into a pillar that is "strong, firm, and steadfast."

It's a part of God's sovereignty that always brings hope and encouragement, and it never fails to astound me.

---

7   1 Peter 5:6-7,10.

Chapter 5

Terror, Trash-Talk, or Trust?
Sovereignty and Our Strengths

Imagine you're living in the Middle East around 1000 BC. The Bronze Age is giving way to the Iron Age, and weapons are more dangerous and prolific than ever.

But if your name happens to be King David, you're fine. You've got a massive army that includes some of the best fighters in the world—battle-hardened veterans who've won victory after victory.

Then there are your Special Forces guys—men whose exploits would put Rambo to shame. They have strange-sounding names, but you wouldn't dare say that to their faces.

- Jashobeam and Abishai were formidable with their spears. Each was distinguished for singlehandedly killing 300 enemy soldiers in one encounter.
- Benaiah killed a lion in a pit on a snowy day and conquered some of the enemy's mightiest warriors. Once, armed only with a club, he outmaneuvered and killed a 7½-foot Egyptian fighter carrying a huge spear.

- In one particularly fierce battle against the Philistines, Eleazar and David held their ground after the rest of their troops retreated, and still succeeded in routing the enemy.
- Among the Gadite army commanders (whose faces are described as the faces of lions), the least was a match for a hundred, and the greatest for a thousand.

This is a sampling of what's recorded in 1 Chronicles chapters 11 and 12, which describe how David became king of all Israel and made his nation a regional superpower. David himself was a fearless warrior with "giant-killing" on his military record. His mighty men, comprising his elite bodyguard and generals, were the best of the best.

If I put myself in David's shoes, I think I'd feel quite secure about my situation. If anyone had reason to be confident in his strength and resources—to be able to say to the enemy, "Go ahead, make my day"—it was David. But what do we find in his recorded prayers, the Psalms?

He says to the Lord, "Give us aid against the enemy, for human help is worthless."[1]

What's *that* about?

Momentary panic and terror? Did all his mighty men suddenly desert him? Was he "trash-talking" them for some reason, saying he couldn't rely on them anymore? What does he mean when he says human help is worthless?

One clue that this is not just David having a bad day—losing his nerve or losing faith in his soldiers—is that he includes the same words in Psalm 108.

---

1   Psalm 60:11.

No, this wasn't a cry of despair. This was David's expression of ultimate trust in God, recognizing that regardless of his strength, it was God who made the difference.

So then, why would he go to the trouble of gathering an army of mighty soldiers and training them to be powerful and effective? We could ask the same question of ourselves: If it's God who makes the difference, why bother with training, education, defence, mobilization, acquiring strength and expertise—or preparation of any kind?

The answer has to do with God's intention when he created us. He could have set up humanity on Earth and left us to fend for ourselves. Alternatively, he could have created us as robots that operated only at the direction of the Programmer while he manipulated every factor involved.

Instead, he created us to function in partnership with him, meaning we are to develop the intellect, strengths, and creative talents he's given us, but never to rely on them as our ultimate answer.

David's use of hyperbole in stating "human help is worthless" was his way of saying to God, "Our strengths and abilities are nothing compared to yours. We'll be as prepared as possible, we'll put our lives on the line and fight with courage and skill, but I know the outcome is in your hands."

For all of David's faults (and there were more than a few), he had a firm grasp on God's sovereignty, and he would not let go. Maybe it was that combination of humility and faith—a strong, active, talented man putting his trust in God—that was the basis for God calling him "a man after my own heart."

It's hard to overstate how unusual this is. Trusting God when we're at our weakest is more common. Fully trusting God when we're strong—whether militarily, financially, physically, intellectually, or spiritually—is rare.

Like David, we must be diligent and fight our battles with perseverance. But it's not ultimately a matter of self-effort. As Scripture encourages us:

> Continue to work out your salvation with fear and trembling, for it is God who works in you to will and to act in order to fulfill his good purpose.[2]

In both of David's Psalms where he says, "human help is worthless," he follows it up with this declaration: "With God we will gain the victory, / and *he* will trample down our enemies."[3]

Regardless of our strength (or lack of it), when we work and train and wage our battles in partnership with him, we can entrust the outcome into the hands of a faithful, sovereign God.

---

2   Philippians 2:12-13.

3   Psalm 60:12; 108:13 (emphasis added).

Chapter 6

To Judge or Not to Judge?
Sovereignty and Judging (Part 1)

One of the famous stories Jesus told was of a self-righteous Pharisee who went to pray in the temple.

The Pharisee noticed that a tax collector was there as well—someone far below himself in terms of moral status. Tax collectors were viewed not only as collaborators with the Romans but also as thieves who overcharged taxes to line their pockets. Pharisees, on the other hand, were considered scrupulous law keepers.

Naturally, the Pharisee thought he could make good use of the comparison in his prayer:

> "God, I thank you that I am not like other people—robbers, evildoers, adulterers—or even like this tax collector. I fast twice a week and give a tenth of all I get."
> But the tax collector stood at a distance. He would not even look up to heaven, but beat his breast and said, "God, have mercy on me, a sinner."[1]

---

1   Luke 18:11-13.

In the Pharisee's mind, God would be impressed by the contrast between the righteous Pharisee and the sinner. But Jesus said it was the *second* man, the tax collector, who went home justified before God, adding that all who justify themselves will be humbled, and those who humble themselves will be exalted.[2]

What was the point of the parable?

Luke records that Jesus told it to those who were confident of their own righteousness and looked down on everyone else. In other words, he was warning us against looking at others and thinking we're better than they are. Another word for that is *judging*.

And what's so wrong about judging?

The word judging is used in more than one way in the Bible. What we're focusing on here is comparing ourselves to others, which typically includes one or more of the following pitfalls:

- Thinking that our good deeds can earn God's favor, especially if (in our humble opinion) they outweigh our failures.
- Pride: thinking we're better than others.
- Assuming that we would do better than someone else if we were in their shoes.

The third point relates directly to God's sovereignty and our limited knowledge. Only God knows what each person contends with in terms of upbringing, personality, temperament, spiritual bondage, trauma, abuse, childhood influences, opportunities (or lack thereof), experiences of pain and loss, and other unique circumstances.

The truth is that we really have no idea whether we'd do better than someone else if we were in their shoes.

If that isn't enough incentive to refrain from judging, let's consider the following commands from Jesus and his apostles:

---

2   Luke 18:14.

- Jesus: "Do not judge, or you too will be judged."[3]
- Paul: "Who are you to judge someone else's servant?"[4]
- James: "But you—who are you to judge your neighbor?"[5]

The more we understand God's sovereignty, the more reasons we find to humble ourselves, both in relation to God and others.

But there is another kind of judging the Bible says we *should* do.

People sometimes quote Jesus's words "Do not judge" when they're doing something wrong and don't want anyone to challenge them. However, Jesus also told us to confront our spiritual brothers or sisters if they sin.[6] Is that even possible without judging?

And the apostle Paul criticized church members at Corinth for suing each other in court instead of finding a wise person within the church to adjudicate—that is, to judge—their dispute.[7]

So, what is the difference?

Without getting too technical, the original New Testament Greek words for judging include meanings like investigating an issue, discerning what is involved, evaluating evidence, and deciding a question.

What is clear is that God, in his sovereignty, assigns some judging to us while reserving certain kinds of judgment to himself, especially when supernatural knowledge is required—like the ability to see into someone's heart.

We may *think* we know someone's motivation or heart attitude, but we don't. Neither do we have the knowledge (or the right) to make comparative judgments between ourselves and others. We're

---

3   Matthew 7:1.

4   Romans 14:4.

5   James 4:12.

6   Matthew 18:15-17.

7   1 Corinthians 6:1-6.

just too subjective in our perspective and too limited in our knowledge. That's God's sovereign territory.

At other times, though, we know something is wrong based on what Jesus taught, but rationalize the wrongdoing either because we're not ready to face the truth in ourselves—or because we're avoiding a possible backlash from others if we were to confront them.

If I'm honest with myself, I have to admit it's easy to slip into the wrong kind of judging—the kind where I harbor critical thoughts or make snide comments—while neglecting the right kind of judging.

Only Jesus consistently got it right: extending mercy to sinners who humbled themselves, but faithfully confronting those who were excusing sin or thought they were better than others. He was—and always is—full of grace and truth.[8]

And the good news? He's working on us to become more like him!

---

8   John 1:14.

Chapter 7

Judge, Jury, and Executioner
Sovereignty and Judging (Part 2)

Confession time: There is one person I tend to judge more than anyone else. This is someone who's offended me more often than I can remember, someone I find difficult to forgive because he can be so irrational and foolish, and all too often he repeats mistakes instead of learning from them.

If you guessed I was talking about myself, you would be correct.

Recently when I was rummaging through an old box from storage, I came across a formal evaluation (review) of an organization I had led many years ago. There were a variety of comments, insights, and recommendations, but instinctively I found myself focusing on the problems they identified, particularly anything related to my role.

Despite it being a long time ago and the fact that those years were a positive experience overall, I found it a little unsettling to read these long-forgotten comments. After a couple of days when I had regained some perspective, I jotted down the following observation:

We're all a mixture of stuff that could be commended or criticized. Accordingly, farewells and funerals will draw out the former, and reviews/evaluations the latter.[1]

If ever I were tempted to play judge, jury, and executioner, it would be in relation to things I've said or done (or not done). And I tend to think I have a *right* to judge myself that way. After all, *I should have known better*, or *I should have learned by now*, or *I really expected more from myself*.

I could even quote Scriptures that speak of judging ourselves. But then I also read what Paul says in his letter to the Corinthians: "I care very little if I am judged by you or by any human court; indeed, I do not even judge myself…It is the Lord who judges me."[2]

Now, if anyone had the capacity to judge himself, I would have thought it would be Paul. He was steeped in Scripture, he was intelligent, honest, and self-aware. Why would Paul avoid self-judgment?

Firstly, he recognized God's sovereignty: that God alone knows us completely and therefore knows how to judge us rightly. And by rightly, I mean with justice, truth, mercy, grace, and redemptive timing.

Secondly, Paul knew how subjective human judgment can be, especially when it has to do with ourselves. We tend to either rationalize our behavior when we should be repenting, or else slip into self-condemnation, which often leaves us in despair.

Thirdly, he knew that he no longer belonged to himself, but to Christ. He goes on to tell the Corinthians, "You are not your own;

---

1   A Biblical example would be how David spoke after the death of his enemy, King Saul, honoring him without mentioning his many flaws (2 Samuel chapter 1). When it comes to reviews and evaluations, however, the approach is more like the one your dentist takes when he probes your teeth and gums: the focus is on finding problems and then considering solutions.

2   1 Corinthians 4:3-4.

36

you were bought at a price."[3] In other words, he understood that he had no more right to judge himself (in the condemning or comparing sense of the word) than he had to judge others that way.

While Paul didn't judge himself, he also didn't buy into the mindset of the self-esteem movement. He didn't write to the Corinthians or the Ephesians or the Romans that they could be anything they wanted to be, and that everything they did was OK.

In fact, he warned against the dangers of egotism:

> For by the grace given me I say to every one of you: Do not think of yourself more highly than you ought, but rather think of yourself with sober judgment, in accordance with the faith God has distributed to each of you.[4]

"With sober judgment…" As opposed to our judgment when we're intoxicated with delusions of grandeur or else wallowing in the depths of despair.

Easier said than done.

In fact, in order to live with a sober judgment of ourselves, we need ongoing exposure to the objective Word of God (Scripture), constant direction and encouragement from the Holy Spirit, and frequent input from those around us.

Given the mixed bag of social media and entertainment on our screens that feature an unending cast of characters we can compare ourselves to, the goal of living with sober judgment of ourselves is more challenging than ever.

It's also a long-term project—at least it is in my case. In preparing this chapter I came across something I had written decades ago—a journal entry stating that I was giving up *the practice of judging myself,*

---

3   1 Corinthians 6:19-20.

4   Romans 12:3.

which has to do with introspection, self-condemnation, rationalization, and self-evaluation.

I went on to say, *By God's grace, I will leave the judging to my Lord and trust the Holy Spirit to bring the approval, correction, and encouragement I need.*

It's time for me to renew that commitment. How about you?

Chapter 8

My Best Executive Decision
Sovereignty and Direction (Part 1)

In the year before I retired, I started thinking about succession planning—how to prepare the organization for new leadership. And so I carefully (and confidentially) began drawing up plans for how such a transition might occur, along with a projected time line.

What actually happened was quite different.

I had been serving as CEO of a long-term healthcare and housing organization that included 700 residents living on campus, a staff of 600, and about 150 volunteers.[1] Given our profile as a Christian organization that was both government-funded and privately financed, it was important to maintain stability—an even keel—so I kept my retirement plans to myself and a few trusted colleagues.

Long-term care in British Columbia is highly regulated, and I was no stranger to reports of all kinds—whether required by a department of the provincial or federal government, Accreditation

---

1   Menno Place, Abbotsford, BC. Website: www.mennoplace.ca .

Canada, or the regional health authority responsible for funding and verifying quality of care.

It was during this time that I received the results of a review of one of our care facilities by the health region—a review that disturbed me, not because it identified some clinical issues for improvement (a valid concern), but because I suspected there was another agenda at play.[2] Having spent three decades in the healthcare system and being familiar with its politics, I "smelled a rat."

During the 20-minute walk home from my office that day, I fumed over the biased nature of the report and the transparent power play involved. But at some point, I made the decision *not* to give in to feelings of anger and frustration, nor to focus on defending our position, but instead to pray.

That was one of the best decisions I ever made.

Later, while I was praying—literally on my knees on this occasion—I believe I heard direction from God that would affect my future, my wife and family, and hundreds of people in my workplace.

That direction was different from my earlier retirement plan, which would have involved a lengthy notice period and months of advertising and recruitment, followed by candidate interviews and eventual hiring by the Board of Directors.

Instead of a potential year of transition, I felt the Lord was advising a notice period closer to three months, which would be feasible if an Interim CEO were hired in the fall. I believe God even gave me the idea to contact a colleague that evening—one of the most respected leaders in British Columbia's healthcare field, a man of Christian character and faith—to see if he would be willing and able to take on such a role, which he was.

---

2   Namely, a personnel issue. (This was neither the review nor the organization referred to in a previous chapter.)

Of course, it was a surprise to the Board, but they subsequently approved the plan, and it all worked out better than I'd expected.

But it wasn't just the organization and those it served who benefited.

A month after the big retirement party in the fall, I got the news that my wife was suffering from pancreatic cancer. As in many cases of this type of cancer, the symptoms had been generic enough that not even the doctors had suspected the underlying cause until it was too late for surgery. But, of course, God knew what was going on.

I realize that, on the face of it, receiving such a diagnosis at that point in a couple's life could seem cruel in its timing. We saw it very differently.

Had I not been free from responsibilities at work—had the Lord not helped me make the right executive decision—I could not have spent those last eleven months with my wife, provided the help and care she needed, and cherished each day we had left. It was a gift for which I will always be grateful.

There was even a bonus.

Since Margarete loved the city, we had planned on moving to Vancouver when I retired. After getting the diagnosis of terminal cancer, we initially thought we we'd have to give up that dream. But, to our surprise, when we prayed about it, God seemed to indicate we should go ahead, so we did.

We found an apartment to lease near the seawall at English Bay, just two blocks from Stanley Park. Located on the 24th floor, we had a view of the Pacific Ocean, Stanley Park, the West End, and the North Shore mountains. It was a wonderful provision from a loving Heavenly Father.

We don't know much about the future, and therefore our plans may or may not be doable, but we have a God who is Sovereign—a Father who knows everything that's coming our way, and who's willing to direct us if we ask him.

I'll close this chapter with one of my favorite Scriptures on the subject of God's sovereign direction:

Trust in the Lord with all your heart

and lean not on your own understanding;
in all your ways submit to him,
and he will make your paths straight.[3]

---

3   Proverbs 3:5-6.

Chapter 9

Beetles and Betelgeuse
Sovereignty and Direction (Part 2)

Did you know that the lowly dung beetle uses the Milky Way stars for navigation?[1]

According to *National Geographic*, dung beetle researchers (yes, believe it or not, there are such scientists) have been able to establish that these insects travel in a straight line by orienting themselves to the light of the stars in our galaxy—one of the brightest of which, oddly enough, is named Betelgeuse.[2]

I find that amazing. Actually, I think it's quite stupendous. We live in a time when we see more of the greatness of our Creator than any generation in history.

But there's also a parallel application that comes to mind. In the Sermon on the Mount, Jesus told us not to worry about what we would eat, drink, or wear, and he used nature to illustrate his point:

---

1   https://blog.nationalgeographic.org/2013/01/24/
    dung-beetles-navigate-via-the-milky-way-first-known-in-animal-kingdom/.

2   Commonly pronounced "beetle-juice."

Look at the birds of the air; they do not sow or reap or store away in barns, and yet your heavenly Father feeds them. Are you not much more valuable than they?"[3]

Had his first century audience known about galaxies and dung beetle research, Jesus might have added: *Consider the dung beetle. If your heavenly Father gives them guidance using the stars of the Milky Way, won't he give you the direction you need? Are you not much more valuable than they?*

How could anyone argue with that? (Mind you, I am assuming that even people with low self-esteem would not sink below "dung beetle level" in their self-judgment.) The point is: God provides for all of his creation, from the least to the greatest, and he encourages us to trust him for the direction we need.

But when we turn to God for direction, we need to remember the vast difference between his wisdom and ours. As parents, we recall times when our young children would get upset because they didn't understand what was going on. It was beyond them because their brains were undeveloped and their frame of reference too limited.

Do we imagine that the gap between our level of understanding and God's level is *less* than that between a parent and a small child?

The Bible says we've been made in the image of God—and thus have the capacity to reason, to imagine, to create, and to make choices—but we still understand very little compared to our Creator. Science has made huge advances in our lifetime, but even then, we find every discovery that provides one answer simply raises a whole new series of questions.

It's as if reality were a thousand-piece puzzle and we're holding just three pieces. Whatever the actual ratio of pieces to the whole puzzle might be, we're seeing only a small part of the picture—which is why we desperately need God's guidance.

---

3   Matthew 6:26-27.

Thankfully, he is able and willing to give us direction when we ask—as we see in this amazing promise from the Psalms: "I will instruct you and teach you in the way you should go; / I will counsel you with my loving eye on you."[4]

One condition for receiving such direction is sincerity or, more precisely, single-mindedness, as we see in this conditional promise in Scripture:

> If any of you lacks wisdom, you should ask God, who gives generously to all without finding fault, and it will be given to you. But when you ask, you must believe and not doubt, because the one who doubts is like a wave of the sea, blown and tossed by the wind. That person should not expect to receive anything from the Lord. Such a person is double-minded and unstable in all they do.[5]

That language can sound a little harsh, but in reality it's designed to help us. There have been many times when it's kept me from getting mired in second-guessing and doubt.

We also are encouraged to be whole-hearted in our approach. The prophet Jeremiah quotes God as saying, "You will seek me and find me when you seek me with all your heart."[6] To underline the point that it's never a waste of time to do that, God says through Isaiah, "I have not said to Jacob's descendants, / 'Seek me in vain.'"[7]

In short, God promises that if we seek him with singleness of heart, we *will* find him and receive the direction we need—and that seeking him is never a useless exercise.

---

4   Psalm 32:8.

5   James 1:5-8.

6   Jeremiah 29:13.

7   Isaiah 45:19.

The God who created lowly dung beetles with the ability to find direction by aligning with the stars (connecting the dots in their own little way) has also made a way for us to find direction in life. It's as simple as seeking him, believing that he will give us wisdom when we ask in faith, and humbly acknowledging his sovereignty.

The Psalmist says, "You guide me with your counsel, / and afterward you will take me into glory."[8]

It's a promise for all of life. Until the day we die.

---

8   Psalm 73:24.

Chapter 10

Carpe Diem!
Sovereignty and Ambition

The Bible doesn't pretend that God's people of old were always saintly. But that fact can be oddly encouraging. When we see their flaws—and the fact that God still used them and helped them mature—it gives us hope for ourselves.

The twelve disciples of Christ, for example, had regular debates about which of them was the greatest. On one of those occasions, it seems they were too embarrassed to admit it:

> They came to Capernaum. When he [Jesus] was in the house, he asked them, "What were you arguing about on the road?" But they kept quiet because on the way they had argued about who was the greatest.[1]

---

1   Mark 9:33-34.

Luke's Gospel tells us that this debate continued up to and including the Last Supper, even though Jesus had talked to them about it before.[2]

So—is ambition wrong?

Not necessarily. But there's a difference between ambition arising out of pride, arrogance, or selfishness, and ambition that's fueled by God's gifts and his Spirit.

We see evidence of gifting and vision among the twelve disciples, but it was mixed with ideas about leadership that still reflected the world around them. Then, as now, leaders typically would lord it over others and expect to be served by them.

Which is why, at the Last Supper, Jesus asserted his sovereignty but then dramatically demonstrated what servant leadership actually looked like:

> Jesus knew that the Father had put all things under his power, and that he had come from God and was returning to God; so he got up from the meal, took off his outer clothing, and wrapped a towel around his waist. After that, he poured water into a basin and began to wash his disciples' feet, drying them with the towel that was wrapped around him.
>
> "Do you understand what I have done for you?" he asked them. "You call me 'Teacher' and 'Lord,' and rightly so, for that is what I am. Now that I, your Lord and Teacher, have washed your feet, I have set you an example that you should do as I have done for you."[3]

Anyone walking roads in Israel at that time would have encountered plenty of dust and manure; thus the washing of guests' feet

---

2   Matthew 20:20-28; Luke 9:46-48; Luke 22:24-30.

3   John 13:3-5;12-15.

was a common courtesy, but relegated to the lowliest servant. That, of course, was the point of Jesus's extraordinary act of humility in washing their feet.

He doesn't tell his disciples they shouldn't aspire to leadership. But he wanted them to understand what that should look like: "Anyone who wants to be first must be the very last, and the servant of all."[4]

The disciples may have argued later whether Jesus intended the foot-washing lesson to be literal or figurative, but either way, the message was clear. Ambition in itself was fine, provided those who aspired to leadership understood the cost: the greater the position, the deeper the commitment to serving.

In the end, many of these disciples, along with Paul and other leaders, showed that they got the message, and even paid the ultimate price as martyrs.

There is one aspect of ambition we don't often think of—the fact that fame and influence last only for a time. And that God's sovereignty is involved both in the rise and the decline of prominence.

When Jesus began his ministry, some of John the Baptist's disciples noticed a worrying trend. People who used to be part of *their* circle were leaving to join Jesus. Here is how John responded to their concerns:

> A person can receive only what is given them from heaven. You yourselves can testify that I said, "I am not the Messiah but am sent ahead of him."
> He must become greater; I must become less.[5]

John the Baptist's ambition was not to become the best-known prophet of the first century. His goal was to prepare the way for the

---

4   Mark 9:35.

5   John 3:27-28, 30.

Messiah and, at the right time, to step away from the spotlight so that Jesus could take his rightful place.

Coming back to John's statement—"A person can receive only what is given them from heaven"—there's a sense in which, because of free will, we can grasp for something else, but why would we? There is nothing higher, wiser, better, or more fulfilling than God's plan for our lives. (Granted, there are times when we struggle to believe that, but if God is sovereign and good, there can be no other conclusion.)

A final thought on the subject of ambition. Welcoming God's sovereignty should never be confused with passivity on our part. As the "father of modern missions," William Carey, famously said, "Expect great things from God; attempt great things for God."

Some might think, *If I had great talent, maybe I could do great things too.* But most of those who accomplished great things in God's kingdom over the centuries have been ordinary people—as were most of the disciples in Jesus's day.

The imprint of our Creator on the most ordinary man or woman is so powerful that, in the hands of God and empowered by his Spirit, he or she can accomplish truly great things.

Ambition? I believe God would say to each of us, "Trust me, follow Jesus's example, serve others, and carpe diem (seize the day)!"

Chapter 11

Impossible Forgetfulness
Sovereignty and Forgiveness (Part 1)

I have always enjoyed those drawings of *impossible objects*—impossible stairs, cubes, and triangles—conceived by brilliant (and slightly twisted) minds like mathematician Roger Penrose or Dutch artist M.C. Escher.

They hint at something beyond our space-and-time world, which makes them intriguing, but a bit unsettling too.

Some people even invent "impossible" propositions: Could an infinitely powerful God create a rock that was too heavy for him to carry? We may spot the flaws in that line of reasoning, but what about this: Can a sovereign, all-knowing God actually forgive *and forget* our sins?

Maybe there's another question we need to address first. Is forgiving and forgetting just a nice idea introduced by one of the kindlier New Testament writers? Not at all. It's first announced by Old Testament prophets. Here is how Isaiah quotes the Lord:

I, even I, am he who blots out
   your transgressions, for my own sake,

and remembers your sins no more.[1]

Referring to the new covenant, Jeremiah records God saying, "For I will forgive their wickedness / and will remember their sins no more,"[2] which is quoted twice in the New Testament.[3]

And the prophet Micah states:

You will again have compassion on us;

> you will tread our sins underfoot
>
> and hurl all our iniquities into the depths of the sea.[4]

Profoundly and poetically stated! But is the truth about God forgiving and forgetting our sins just poetic license?

As we grapple with what that really means, let's consider for a moment what it *cannot* mean. It cannot mean that God is oblivious to what's going on in our lives.

Suppose I am struggling with drug addiction, and each time I fall, I sincerely confess my failure and ask God for forgiveness. Would God be unaware of my drug habit because I've confessed each time? Of course not. Otherwise he couldn't help me.

So, what does forgetting mean in this case? It means he's not holding our sins against us. To quote another Old Testament prophet, "None of the sins that person has committed will be remembered against them."[5]

That can be a challenge if we apply it our interpersonal relationships. After repeated offences, we tend to get fed up and say, "Look, this is the tenth time you've done this!" promptly forgetting that godly love "keeps no record of wrongs."[6]

---

1   Isaiah 43:25.

2   Jeremiah 31:34.

3   Hebrews 8:12, 10:17.

4   Micah 7:19.

5   Ezekiel 33:16.

6   1 Corinthians 13:5.

But when God forgives, it's different. I'll refer again to a key verse from the book of James: "If any of you lacks wisdom, you should ask God, who gives generously to all without finding fault, and it will be given to you."[7]

I really appreciate the phrase "without finding fault." A literal translation is *does not reproach.*

Most of us can relate to the experience of feeling hesitant to approach God when we're in trouble, afraid that he'll bring up the dumb mistakes we made or the sins we committed that landed us in such a mess. But the Bible clearly tells us that when we repent and receive his forgiveness, he doesn't remember our sins against us. Neither does he reproach us when we go to him for wisdom at such times, saying, "I told you so."

And it's not because he doesn't take sin seriously.

The sin he laid on Jesus at the crucifixion—that is, *our* sin—was so horrible, so revolting, that he had to turn his face away from his only Son at that moment, and Jesus cried out, "My God, my God, why have you forsaken me?"[8]

We cannot for a moment equate God's forgetting our sin with the idea that sin is not a big deal. But neither should we make the mistake of thinking his forgiveness is grudgingly given, as if he's keeping track of it in some divine ledger, ready to throw our misdeeds in our face.

Here is how writer Mike Mason describes it:

> As Christians we trust that even now God has not only forgiven our sin, He has forgotten all about it. We believe this even though we cannot grasp it. How, we wonder, could God ever really forget anything? But He has, He has! He forgot all our sin when He took it into Himself on the cross.

---

7   James 1:5.

8   Matthew 27:46.

He forgot it when He said, "I'm thirsty," and instead of cool water the bitter cup of evil was raised to His lips and He drank it down to the dregs. And then He died with all of the world's shadows inside Him. He took them down to Hell and left them there.[9]

A holy and sovereign God who forgives and forgets? I can't help but think of Jesus's words when he said, "What is impossible with man is possible with God."[10]

Barney Coombs, a treasured spiritual father in my life, once spoke an unforgettable word of encouragement to me. He's with the Lord now, but that resonant voice and English accent remain fresh in my memory as he said, "Art, *bask in the imputed righteousness of Christ.*"

If he were still here, I'd say, "I'll do that, Barney, knowing that God graciously forgives and forgets."

---

9   Mike Mason, *The Gospel According to Job*, rev. ed. (1994; repr., Wheaton, Ill: Crossway, 2002), 422.

10   Luke 18:27.

Chapter 12

The Inexcusable
Sovereignty and Forgiveness (Part 2)

For years I followed the "Adam" model whenever I knowingly did something wrong: I would try to hide from God.

The reasons were probably the same as any other guilty person: I felt too unworthy to approach God at that point and, besides, I figured he'd be upset with me for a while. What I didn't understand was how God's sovereignty relates to forgiveness.

First of all, it's God's sovereign *choice* to forgive. He's under no obligation to forgive anyone or anything, and we could never earn forgiveness—not even if we worked at it all our lives.

Sin can be atoned for only by the sacrifice of a perfect life. In the Old Testament, it was (symbolically) a lamb without imperfections, which is why Jesus is referred to as "the Lamb of God who takes away the sin of the world."

God made a once-for-all-time choice when he sent Jesus to bear the penalty of our sin. Sin truly is paid for—in a way that we cannot add to through good deeds or even by repenting more earnestly.

(That's not to downplay the value of repentance and restitution, but these have nothing to do with actual payment for sin.)

On that basis alone, there is no point in waiting to re-establish our relationship with God after we've sinned. There's absolutely nothing we can do to make ourselves more acceptable to him. We approach God solely on the basis of Jesus's sacrifice.

And that's why we need to rethink the "time" issue in forgiveness. On a human level, the passage of time does make a difference when someone offends us, because it takes us a while to process things and come to a place of being willing to forgive.

It doesn't work that way with God. We don't need to wait for him to cool down, or allow time to elapse so that the wrongdoing doesn't seem quite as bad, or wait until we've had a chance to do some good deeds to "balance out" the sin. No amount of time and no amount of good works will make a shred of difference in the forgiveness of that sin.

In fact, the only person who gains when we keep our distance from God is the enemy of our souls. That truth alone has been enough to motivate me to reconnect with God when feeling particularly unworthy.

Worthiness, of course, has nothing to do with our feelings and everything to do with the value God places on us. And when that value is the very life of his Son Jesus Christ, there is nothing more we can add.

As noted earlier, God's forgiveness is his choice, a choice demonstrated in the life and death of Jesus. But his sovereignty also means that whatever he tells us to do is non-optional. Here's what Jesus said about forgiveness after teaching *The Lord's Prayer:*

> For if you forgive other people when they sin against you, your heavenly Father will also forgive you. But if you do

not forgive others their sins, your Father will not forgive your sins.[1]

Given the clarity of that teaching, I think it would be dangerous to assume there are exceptions to the rule. If I want to be forgiven, I have to forgive others. And if that seems an insurmountable challenge, I may need to seek advice from someone who has worked through bitterness and resentment to get to a place of peace and forgiveness.

A helpful perspective on this subject is found in Jesus's parable of the unmerciful servant,[2] a lesson that could be summed up in this simple statement from C.S. Lewis: "To be a Christian means to forgive the inexcusable because God has forgiven the inexcusable in you."[3]

Finally, we know the Bible tells us that God forgives and forgets, but is that also possible for *us*?

We're neither robots nor God, which means that forgiveness is usually a process. It takes time for painful feelings to be healed, for damage to be repaired, for restitution to be made, for reconciliation to be completed, and for trust to be restored.

When we've been wronged, memories of that offence often return, and when they do, we must keep choosing to extend forgiveness. We may not be capable of entirely *forgetting* an offence, but God doesn't want us to keep a record of wrongs[4]—no secret videos stored in our memory for use if and when needed as ammunition.

In the Sermon on the Mount, Jesus tells us to love our enemies, to do good to those who hate us, to bless those who curse us, and

---

1   Matthew 6:14-15.

2   Matthew 18:21-35.

3   C.S. Lewis, *The Weight of Glory* (New York: HarperCollins, 2001; originally published 1949), 158.

4   1 Corinthians 13:5.

to pray for those who mistreat us.[5] That kind of response takes a sovereign work of grace; it's something that's only possible with God.

We live in a world full of people who need forgiveness. Because of God's sovereign choice to forgive, we're free! Like Adam, we can emerge from hiding. We can live free from bitterness and resentment, and we can overcome curses with blessing.

---

5   Luke 6:27-28.

Chapter 13

Choosing Our Fears
Sovereignty and Fear (Part 1)

There's an old sketch by comedian Bob Newhart that's made the rounds for years on YouTube called "Stop It!" Playing the role of a psychiatrist, Newhart takes an unusually simple approach to complex psychiatric problems, and charges only $5 per session. After the patient painstakingly describes her hang-ups and phobias, he gives his professional answer in just two words: "Stop it!"

We laugh because it's such a ludicrous response, carried out with Newhart's classic deadpan demeanor. But as absurd as that approach may be, there's a kernel of truth in it—namely that fear involves a *choice*.

Among the many instructions in the Bible, the one repeated most often is "Do not be afraid" (or an equivalent phrase).[1] But why is it stated as a command? Isn't fear an uncontrollable *feeling*?

---

1   https://www1.cbn.com/soultransformation/archive/2011/10/21/fear-not.-365-days-a-year. While some commentators identify 365 such Scriptures, others have narrowed it down to "only" 136.

The truth is: we do make choices regarding fear. And how we choose will have a huge impact on our lives and on others. King Saul, Israel's first king, ultimately was rejected by God when he gave in to fear and disobeyed the prophet's instructions.[2]

In the book of Jeremiah, we find one of the most dramatic stories of fear and disobedience in the Bible. It's a time of great danger for the Jews that remained in Judah during the Babylonian exile, especially after someone assassinated the governor that Babylon had appointed.

Chapters 42 and 43 describe how the Jewish leaders approach the prophet Jeremiah. They're afraid, and many are saying they should seek asylum in Egypt, but they tell Jeremiah they'll do whatever God says: "Whether it is favorable or unfavorable, we will obey the Lord our God, to whom we are sending you, so that it will go well with us, for we will obey the Lord our God."[3]

Ten days go by—days during which there must have been constant speculation and worry. And when Jeremiah finally comes back to them with God's word not to flee to Egypt, they promptly reject his word and give in to their fears—with disastrous results.

Interestingly enough, when Jeremiah was called to be a prophet to the nations, he himself was strongly warned about giving in to fear, especially fear of the people. God said, "Do not be terrified by them, or I will terrify you before them."[4]

God also spoke plainly to the prophet Isaiah regarding fear:

Do not call conspiracy
    everything this people calls a conspiracy;
do not fear what they fear,
    and do not dread it.

---

2   1 Samuel 13.

3   Jeremiah 42:6.

4   Jeremiah 1:17.

The Lord Almighty is the one you are to regard holy,
> he is the one you are to fear,
> he is the one you are to dread.[5]

Jesus had a very similar message when he taught his disciples:

> I tell you, my friends, do not be afraid of those who kill the body and after that can do no more. But I will show you whom you should fear: Fear him who, after your body has been killed, has authority to throw you into hell. Yes, I tell you, fear him. Are not five sparrows sold for two pennies? Yet not one of them is forgotten by God. Indeed, the very hairs of your head are all numbered. Don't be afraid; you are worth more than many sparrows.[6]

In other words, people who threaten us physically may be scary, but they can't touch our eternal life. God, on the other hand, is to be regarded with reverence, awe, and respect because of his holiness and sovereign power. And he is to be trusted because he watches over us and is aware of the tiniest details of our lives—even the number of hairs on our head!

Rob Reimer, founder of the Soul Care course, offers these helpful insights:

We can either act on fear or we can act on faith, but we cannot act on both.

> David had an unusually wise understanding of the things of the soul. He made the connection between fear and disobedience, fear and soul disasters, fear and lost destinies. He probably learned this lesson by watching Saul lose his kingdom over fear...David knew that if fear lurked in his

---

5   Isaiah 8:12-13.

6   Luke 12:4-7.

heart unattended, it could cost him immeasurably, so he prayed about it.[7]

We find the words of his prayer in one of the Psalms:
Search me, God, and know my heart;
test me and know my anxious thoughts.[8]
In an age of information overload, replete with fake news, scaremongering, and conspiracy theories, God wants us to think and act in a way that is different from the world around us.

We are not to fear what others fear. If we're doing that, we need to "stop it!"—and instead fear God, ask him to check out our hearts, and put our trust in him.[9]

---

7   Rob Reimer, *Soul Care* (Franklin, Tennessee: Carpenter's Son Publishing, 2016), 187.

8   Psalm 139:23.

9   No extra charge for that advice!

Chapter 14

Dullards in the Storm
Sovereignty and Fear (Part 2)

My computer screensaver is a shot I took of the Sea of Galilee during a tour of Israel. The water is perfectly calm while shafts of sunlight pierce the clouds as if radiating from heaven itself.

But it's a lake with a reputation for sudden, violent storms, and one of those churned up many years ago while Jesus and his disciples were crossing it. Here's how the story is told in Mark's Gospel:

> A furious squall came up, and waves broke over the boat, so that it was nearly swamped. Jesus was in the stern, sleeping on a cushion. The disciples woke him and said to him, "Teacher, don't you care if we drown?"
>
> He got up, rebuked the wind and said to the waves, "Quiet! Be still!" Then the wind died down and it was completely calm.
>
> He said to his disciples, "Why are you so afraid? Do you still have no faith?"

They were terrified and asked each other, "Who is this? Even the wind and the waves obey him!"[1]

First the disciples were fearful due to the sudden storm; then they were terrified when Jesus calmed the storm by a verbal command.

Jesus wasn't impressed, asking them why they were so afraid, and suggesting it was due to their lack of faith. He rebukes not only the wind and the waves, but also his disciples' response.

And this wasn't the only time. During one teaching session when Jesus told a parable, Peter says, "Explain the parable to us." Jesus does so, but first he asks them, "Are you still so dull?"[2]

I can imagine Peter trying to decide whether to answer "yes" or "no," and a sharp jab from James's elbow convincing him to keep quiet and consider it a rhetorical question. (That part is speculation, of course.)

It's encouraging that the Bible includes less-than-complimentary stories about God's people. It gives us hope—because we all act like dullards at times.

But we're all meant to grow out of our fear and into faith, out of our dullness and into clear understanding. Jesus expected his disciples to connect the dots, but all too often they failed to do so.

What dots was Jesus expecting them to connect? We find a clue in the way Jesus responded to envoys from John the Baptist (then imprisoned) who were asking if Jesus was the expected one, the Messiah:

> Go back and report to John what you have seen and heard: The blind receive sight, the lame walk, those who have leprosy are cleansed, the deaf hear, the dead are raised, and the good news is proclaimed to the poor.[3]

---

1   Mark 4:37-41.

2   Matthew 15:15-16.

3   Luke 7:22.

Jesus didn't ask them to believe in him out of blind faith; he wanted them to consider the evidence—comparing the record of his life with what was prophesied about the Messiah in Scripture.

Jesus's disciples had seen that evidence first-hand, so they had no excuse for their panicked reaction in the storm, especially since their miracle-working Master was the one who had initiated the journey and was right there in the boat with them (albeit asleep).

So, what might have been the *right* response to such a crisis?

Our friends in England might suggest something like this: *Sorry to wake you, Master, but we're having a spot of bother with this storm. Would you mind terribly having a quick look and giving us a few pointers on survival at sea?*

But the disciples were not British, and this was no Monty Python sketch. If the right response to crisis is neither panic nor denial, what does the Lord expect? What might faith—rather than fear—look like in this storm scenario? Here are three possible responses:

- *Peter:* "Look, guys, this is a bad situation, but let's wake Jesus. I don't know what he'll do, but he's always had the answer to every problem before, so no need to panic."
- *James:* "Remember that centurion's servant he healed by just saying a word? I'll bet he could command the water in this boat to leave. Maybe he'd even command the wind to settle down."
- *John:* "Why not just let him sleep? There's no question that God sent him, so God also knows how to look after him. And since we're in the same boat with him, we should be just fine."

None of those responses are rocket science, but just ordinary reasoning that even simple fishermen like Peter, James, and John could have managed. Instead, they panicked.

Unlike fear, *faith* is fundamentally logical—provided it's based on the truth of God's sovereignty. If God is all-powerful and all-wise and all-loving, then all is well.

In the words of the Psalmist:

God is our refuge and strength,
>an ever-present help in trouble.
Therefore we will not fear, though the earth give way
>and the mountains fall into the heart of the sea,
though its waters roar and foam
>and the mountains quake with their surging.[4]

During the storms of life, we sometimes forget both the Scriptures and the Person we're with. But Jesus didn't abandon his disciples when they were fearful and dull in spirit, and neither will he abandon us.

He'll patiently teach us until we learn to trust his sovereignty: until we get it. Until we connect the dots.

---

4   Psalm 46:1-3 (emphasis added).

Chapter 15

Seal of Approval
Sovereignty and Humility

I suppose we've all heard about the man who was given a badge of honor for his humility, but then had it taken away because he wore it.

There is something about humility that we're drawn to, yet we also want recognition for who we are and what we do. The result can be a strange mix of striving, embarrassment, and humor.

When one of Winston Churchill's political opponents was being praised as a modest man, Churchill responded with a classic back-handed compliment: "He has much to be modest about."[1]

There is only one person in history who didn't have "much to be modest about," and that's Jesus Christ. But listen to what he says:

> Take my yoke upon you and learn from me, for I am gentle and *humble* in heart, and you will find rest for your souls.[2]

---

1   https://winstonchurchill.org/publications/finest-hour/finest-hour-130/
correct-attributions-or-red-herrings/.

2   Matthew 11:29 (emphasis added).

Then consider this Scripture referring to Jesus: "The Son is the radiance of God's glory and the exact representation of his being."[3] That means if Jesus the Son is humble in heart, God the Father and the God the Holy Spirit are as well!

The sovereign Creator of the universe with its estimated two trillion galaxies,[4] each containing billions (sometimes hundreds of billions) of stars—this Creator is *humble in heart?* Isn't that one of the most stupendous truths imaginable?

Taking this a step further, does it leave any room whatsoever for pride on *anyone's* part?

The Bible hints that pride was the original sin of Lucifer (whom we now know as the devil), a great heavenly being who wanted to be like his Creator—mainly to receive his glory—and then was cast out of heaven.[5] But does that mean the desire for recognition is wrong?

Not at all.

Even Jesus, as a man but also as God's eternal Son, welcomed his Father's recognition. John the Baptist records that an audible voice from heaven was heard at Jesus's baptism, saying, "This is my Son, whom I love; with him I am well pleased."[6]

The problem arises when we seek recognition in the wrong places. A key problem of the religious leaders of that time was that "they loved human praise more than praise from God."[7] Jesus put it very bluntly: "Everything they do is done for people to see."[8]

Quite the indictment. But before I start thinking about how much better I am than those hypocrites, I might consider how

---

3   Hebrews 1:3.

4   https://www.nationalgeographic.com/science/space/universe/galaxies/.

5   See Isaiah 14.

6   Matthew 3:17.

7   John 12:43.

8   Matthew 23:5.

much of what I do is done to please God vs trying to gain other people's approval.

A more subtle mistake is when we look for God's validation (a divine pat on the head) for our performance or achievement. As far as God is concerned, the key issue is our identity as his sons and daughters. It's who we are, not what we do.

The Gospels record a time when Jesus sent out 72 disciples to preach, to heal the sick, and to cast out demons. They were thrilled with the results and told Jesus, "Lord, even the demons submit to us in your name." While Jesus was also pleased, he made a point of telling them, "Do not rejoice that the spirits submit to you, but rejoice that your names are written in heaven."[9]

If we base our value on what we do, we will always struggle with insecurity. Since we're human, our performance level will vary, and soon we start seeing ourselves as winners or failures—with the result being either pride or despondency.

Jesus wants us to rejoice in our identity. Beyond anything else, he wants us to know we have a Father who created us, who knows us personally, who has an eternal destiny planned for us, and who is working in us right now.

Humility is not an add-on virtue. Rather, it's a reflection of God himself, who is "humble in heart." And since we're made in his image and we have his Spirit living in us, we have the privilege of becoming humble in heart too.

How does that happen? I (humbly) submit the following:

- Someone who is humble in heart is not easily offended. That means we can go to God with anything—including our confession of pride and our need for true humility.

---

9   Luke 10:17, 20.

- We can rejoice that our names are recorded in heaven, focusing on our identity as children of God rather than our accomplishments.
- We can purposefully seek God's approval above and beyond anyone else's.
- We can take practical steps to humble ourselves through prayer, fasting, confession, and serving others.

The apostle Peter, who at one time was vying for position among the disciples, wrote this in later years:

> God opposes the proud but shows favor to the humble. Humble yourselves, therefore, under God's mighty hand, that he may lift you up in due time.[10]

Humbling ourselves may not feel good at the time—and may not earn us a badge. But it's the *right* way of becoming more like God.

---

10   1 Peter 5:5-6.

Chapter 16

Recalculating
Sovereignty and Our Mistakes

If you've ever used an audible GPS system in your car, you're familiar with what happens when you go off course.

I don't know what I was expecting the first time that happened to me, but I was pleasantly surprised. There was no annoying buzzer (like the kind that signals a wrong answer on a game show) nor criticism (like "What were you thinking?"). There wasn't even a hint of disappointment in the voice of my GPS guide; just a matter-of-fact, one-word statement—"Recalculating"—followed by a new set of instructions for getting back on course. It seemed positively providential.

Which makes me wonder: how does God deal with our mistakes?

He's not just an oracle handing out dispassionate advice; he's a divine Person who relates to us with emotion. So how does he express himself when we take a wrong turn in life? Does he highlight our immaturity and foolishness and then hammer us for it?

He could do that, of course, but his way is not to shame or condemn, but rather to draw us back with grace and wisdom.

And that applies whether we're just slightly off course or whether we've been going in the wrong direction long enough to get into serious trouble.

If it's the latter, God sometimes does allow us to bear the consequences of our decisions, especially if we need a wake-up call, but his focus is on restoring us—getting us back on track.

He even knows how to clean up our messes and repair what's been damaged. How can we sure of that? Because of verses like this: "And we know that in all things God works for the good of those who love him, who have been called according to his purpose."[1]

That Scripture is so key to understanding God's sovereignty that I'll repeat it from another translation: "And we know that God causes all things to work together for good to those who love God, to those who are called according to His purpose."[2]

So, how does God's sovereignty cover our foolishness? Is he great enough to work *good* out of our mistakes? I believe the "all things" of Romans 8 does mean *all* things. The testimony of God's people throughout history is that there's nothing he can't redeem.

And what about mistakes that can't be undone?

While it is true that some decisions cannot be reversed, there is no such thing as an impossible situation for God. As he said to the prophet Jeremiah, "I am the Lord, the God of all mankind. Is anything too hard for me?"[3]

But even if we accept that a sovereign God knows all things and can do all things, where does that leave us if we think we've made a mistake in something as hugely consequential and irreversible as marriage?

---

1   Romans 8:28 (NIV).

2   Romans 8:28 (NASB).

3   Jeremiah 32:27.

Danny Silk, a Christian marriage and family counselor in California, tells of how he found out years after his wedding that premarital psychological tests suggested he and his fiancée (now wife) were incompatible and should not marry one another. Being unaware of that information, they married and did in fact experience serious trouble in their relationship. But they struggled through it, and in the process developed a course that has helped thousands of other couples.

Jesus speaks of God's involvement whenever a man and woman marry—"What God has joined together, let no one separate"[4]—indicating that God *enters into* a couple's choice and confirms it. Which means that *after* the wedding, any question of whether the marriage was a mistake is no longer relevant.[5]

There are in fact a number of examples in the Bible of God's people making major mistakes regarding marriage (including King David) and yet God worked those things into his plans and purposes.

God is not sitting on the throne of heaven with a worried expression on his face, wondering what he could possibly do about a certain messy situation. Because he exists in eternity and inhabits every dimension of time, he already knows the outcome of every scenario, and knows exactly what to do. He doesn't even have to take time to "recalculate."

What's more, he never abandons us, even when we turn the wrong way. As King David prayed,

Where can I go from your Spirit?

Where can I flee from your presence?

If I rise on the wings of dawn,

---

4   Matthew 19:6.

5   Second-guessing a marriage choice is a temptation we need to resolutely refuse. That said, the Bible does not advocate people being trapped when the marriage covenant is destroyed.

if I settle on the far side of the sea,
  even there your hand will guide me,
    your right hand will hold me fast.[6]

In other words, God will be there at our destination. Sometimes we may hear, "Well done, good and faithful servant." Or, it may be, "Here's where you went off course, but let me show you how we're going to resolve that." Or even, "This situation isn't going to change for a while. It may be painful, but I want you to trust me to deal with it at the right time."

The point is: our mistakes are not the final word. His sovereign, gracious plan (in spite of our blunders) is the true end of the story.

---

6   Psalm 139:7,9-10.

Chapter 17

Bright Hope for Tomorrow
Sovereignty and My Future

The other day I came across some notes I had written shortly before learning that my wife had pancreatic cancer. It was while we were on vacation at the Oregon Coast, in a room overlooking miles of sandy beaches and the massive, surging waves of the Pacific Ocean.

My holiday reading tends to be lighter fare—fiction, science, or sometimes science fiction—as I'm enjoying a break from the weight and complexity of life. But this time, for some reason, I found myself reflecting on a non-lightweight character in the Bible named Job.

It was something he said after he'd lost almost everything—his vast herds, his servants, his ten children, and his health. After sitting in silence with friends who had come to comfort him, Job says, "What I feared has come upon me; what I dreaded has happened to me."[1]

---

1   Job 3:25.

I remember saying to Margarete, "Isn't it scary to think what God allows in the lives of good people?" Then I had jotted down the following notes:

> But, as the story eventually showed, even the best of us have flaws that show up under extreme pressure, and God has ways of dealing with them.
>
> It is indeed scary to think what God may allow, but what are the alternatives? Would the following scenarios be any less scary?
>
> - God indulging our desire to have everything our way (like parents who always allow their toddlers to do what they want) and not disciplining or refining us?
> - God allowing Satan's accusations about our motives for serving God to go unchallenged?[2]
> - God putting our pleasure above his glory (which would make him less than God)?
> - The Creator becoming accountable to the creature?
>
> Any scenario in which God does not act as the all-knowing, all-powerful Sovereign is far scarier than the tragic events that Job endured.
>
> Having said that, God does not want us to live in fear about what could happen. We are not capable of handling knowledge of the future. And, in any case, the long-term future is glorious. Even if we go through massive loss, as Job did, there is restoration at the end, whether in this life or in the next. We can trust the One who holds the future.

That's where my notes ended.

---

2   In Job 1:9-11, Satan suggests that Job fears God only because of the blessings.

Looking back, I'm amazed to see how God was preparing us for what lay ahead. Three months after those musings about Job, the future arrived in the form of a terminal cancer diagnosis.

But God's grace arrived as well—for both of us—in the form of a supernatural peace that was as real as anything we'd ever experienced.

> In an email to family and friends during chemo treatments, Margarete wrote, *I was reminded of the words to a song from several years ago:* My life is in your hands / My heart is in your keeping / I'm never without hope / Not when my future is with you / My life is in your hands / And though I may not see clearly / I will lift my voice and sing / 'Cause your love does amazing things / Lord, I know, my life is in your hands.[3] *That pretty much sums up our faith at this point.*

A few years before that, my pastor, Charlie Whitley, had delivered a sermon inspired by John Piper's book *Future Grace*.[4] It was called "Remembering the Future" (referring to the fact that the Bible tells us, in general terms, what the future looks like), and included ten key points so simple yet so profound that I find I need to regularly remind myself of them:

1. God wins.
2. Those who are on his side also win.
3. Evil does not overwhelm good, but vice versa.
4. Evil is temporary; good is eternal.
5. Relationships change in some ways, but always for the better.

---

3   Kathy Troccoli, *My Life is in Your Hands, Kathy Troccoli* (Brentwood, TN: Reunion Records, 1994). https://www.lyrics.com/lyric/2666647/Kathy+Troccoli/My+Life+Is+in+Your+Hands.

4   John Piper, *Future Grace* (Sisters, Oregon: Multnomah Books, 1995).

6. There is an end to sorrow and disappointment, but no end to joy and fulfillment.

7. Deception and arrogance come to an end; truth and humility remain and flourish.

8. The limitations of this space/time world will come to an end.

9. What is ultimately rewarded is not achievement or success, but rather faithfulness, especially enduring faith.

10. There will be reward and rest in place of frustration and stress.

Our conclusion? Whatever the present may look like, and despite any fears that come to mind about the future, we don't have to anxiously wonder about what might happen, or shudder at the thought of loss or calamity.

We can be at peace because (in the words of an old hymn[5]) we can have "bright hope for tomorrow"—because we have a God who is always loving and absolutely sovereign.

---

5   *Great is Thy Faithfulness,* written by Thomas Chisholm (Public Domain).

Chapter 18

Personal Preference
Sovereignty and God's Messengers

Some people are OK with Jesus, but when it comes to his *representatives*—not so much.

That may seem reasonable enough. But notice what Jesus says to his twelve disciples: "Anyone who welcomes you welcomes me, and anyone who welcomes me welcomes the one who sent me."[1] (Some translations use the term *receives* instead of *welcomes*, but it means the same.)

Jesus said the same thing when he sent out 72 disciples to preach, heal, and cast out demons: "Whoever listens to you listens to me; whoever rejects you rejects me; but whoever rejects me rejects him who sent me."[2]

It's not difficult to imagine how people of that day might have responded to Jesus:

Seriously, Lord? And then the criticisms would start…

---

1   Matthew 10:40.

2   Luke 10:16.

- *Most of your disciples are poorly educated. I asked one of those fishermen-turned-disciples a fairly basic question about Scripture the other day, and he was stumped!*
- *I can't really trust a guy like Levi who was a traitor to Israel by joining the Roman occupation as a tax collector. I'm pretty sure he's still a "Romanophile" at heart.*
- *Simon the Zealot may not be plotting with terrorists against Rome, but he still harbors extreme views. I overheard him the other day and was shocked at his over-the-top political rhetoric.*
- *James and John—those so-called Sons of Thunder—don't know the first thing about mercy. I heard they wanted to call fire down from heaven on a Samaritan village and burn everyone up. That's horrible! And I'm supposed to receive the Gospel from them?*
- *Peter is so unstable. Sometimes he's boasting about being the greatest among the disciples, sometimes he's swearing (like the fisherman he is), and sometimes he's blurting out some amazing truth. How do I know he's on track when he preaches?*
- *Judas Iscariot puts on a good front, but I've heard he pilfers money from the group funds. I don't think I could trust a messenger like that.*
- *None of the disciples has a clear understanding of what the Messiah really is meant to be and do. Why should I pay attention to anyone who has such a limited grasp of theology?*

But Jesus simply says, "Very truly I tell you, whoever accepts anyone I send accepts me; and whoever accepts me accepts the one who sent me."[3] So, if we take him seriously, we cannot reject or

---

3   John 13:20.

discount a message just because the messenger is flawed. The fact is, God has used flawed messengers throughout history and, whether we like it or not, he still does today.

But does that mean we're supposed to accept every televangelist who claims to speak for God? Of course not. Jesus also gave this warning:

> Watch out for false prophets. They come to you in sheep's clothing, but inwardly they are ferocious wolves. By their fruit you will recognize them.[4]

That last line is echoed later in Scripture:

> Remember your leaders, who spoke the word of God to you. *Consider the outcome of their way of life* and imitate their faith.[5]

We are to examine the outcome—the fruit—of a leader's life, which typically is revealed over time.

We're also meant to weigh their message. The Book of Acts speaks approvingly of the Bereans who checked Paul's message against Scripture to make sure it was true.[6] Paul himself warned against people perverting the gospel of Christ, declaring, "But even if we or an angel from heaven should preach a gospel other than the one we preached to you, let them be under God's curse!"[7]

---

4   Matthew 7:15-16.

5   Hebrews 13:7 (emphasis added).

6   Acts 17:11.

7   Galatians 1:8.

If anyone's teaching contradicts basic Scriptural truths,[8] we shouldn't receive it. (But keep in mind that there are plenty of minor doctrinal areas on which Bible-believing Christians differ.[9])

A final point: The Information Age offers an endless supply of messages through books, podcasts, and videos, but what we may forget is that God intends his church to be relational—like family. Note what Paul says to the church in Corinth:

> Even if you had ten thousand guardians in Christ, you do not have many fathers, for in Christ Jesus I became your father through the gospel. Therefore I urge you to imitate me.[10]

Paul knows that the Corinthians have benefited from various ministries, but he encourages them not to forget his role as a spiritual father. Was he vying for special recognition? I don't think so. He was focused on their well-being, and believed they would receive a special grace from God when they listened to his message and followed his example. We too may need to consider that factor in regard to our spiritual fathers.

Some issues in the 21st century are the same as the 1st. We're still faced with the matter of God's sovereignty when it comes to receiving his messengers. Writing off certain ministries based on personal preference, minor differences, or even perceived flaws is not a valid option.

God has the right to say what he wants and through whom he wants to say it. Our part is to welcome the messenger and say "yes" to God.

---

8   Truths accepted by Christians for almost two millennia, such as the Apostles Creed and the Nicene Creed.

9   Romans chapter 14 offers examples of minor doctrinal differences.

10   1 Corinthians 4:15-16.

Chapter 19

The Cost of Relationship
What a Sovereign God Values Most

It's Maundy Thursday, the day before the Easter weekend.

I wasn't sure exactly what to expect to hear from God this morning. Having abandoned the notion of prayer as just a monologue where I would speak and God would listen, I had decided to pray in the form of a two-way conversation while hiking the trails near our home. Jesus did say, after all, "My sheep listen to my voice."[1]

But I have to admit I was hesitant to start the dialogue. It was the continuation of a soul-searching time the day before when I found myself thinking that I really didn't like myself very much.

The reasons were myriad. For one thing, I couldn't think of any area of life where I felt I was doing well. Instead, there was a general sense of failure—or at best mediocrity—regarding what I was expecting of myself or what I believed God expected of me.

During a recent "Hearing God" seminar at our church we were encouraged to ask the Lord, "What do you like about me?" and then

---

1   John 10:27.

write down what we thought we heard him saying. It's an exercise that challenges you to the core.[2]

As I was walking this morning, I thought to myself, *Why should I ask such a question? Why not ask, "What do you dislike about me?" Wouldn't that be more honest, more to the point?*

But as I started up the trail, it seemed like the Lord was asking *me* a question: "How would you respond if your wife or one of your children asked you that?"

Well...

Almost instantly I knew that if a family member were to ask such a question, it would have arisen from feelings of discouragement or rejection, and I would say something like this in reply:

You know, there might come a time when we could talk about such things, but right now, the most important thing for you to know is that I love you unconditionally and that I think you're wonderful!

In other words, I would convey to my loved one that our relationship was of far greater importance than his or her level of performance.

And, just as instantly, I realized that that was exactly how God sees me. He isn't focused first and foremost on my "issues." He isn't problem oriented—because he has the answer to every problem. And he sees relationship as the bigger issue.

As that realization was reverberating in my brain, a Scripture verse came to mind: "For the joy set before him he [Jesus] endured the cross, scorning its shame, and sat down at the right hand of the throne of God."[3]

---

2   "Hearing God" is one of the Church Renewal seminars developed by Southland Church in Manitoba and now used by churches across Canada and beyond.

3   Hebrews 12:2.

Joy? What was that all about? And how could it possibly override the horrors of public execution on a cross?

We know from the Bible that Jesus took joy in pleasing his Father[4] and that he knew he was fulfilling his destiny on earth. But the "joy set before him" also included the prospect of *us*—those who would be set free from sin's domain to become part of God's eternal family.

While the cross eventually became the universal emblem of Christianity, it was very much a symbol of shame in the first century. The Romans had perfected crucifixion as slow torture leading to death, but they also ensured their victims were humiliated by nailing them to a cross naked and placing the execution sites next to public roads. (That became more real to me on our Israel tour as we viewed a likely site of the actual crucifixion. It was still next to a thoroughfare.)

How could Jesus scorn the shame of the cross? The Greek word for scorn means "to despise" or "to think slightly of." It's the same comparative term Jesus used when he said that those who didn't "hate" father, mother, wife, children, brothers, sisters—and even their own life—couldn't be his disciples.[5]

So, through the cross he was saying that he valued his relationship with the Father—*and his relationship with us*—far above his suffering and shame.

That's what we celebrate on Good Friday: the sovereign God taking the form of a human servant. Dying a disgraceful, agonizing death. And thinking we were worth the cost—so much so that he considered the shame "no big deal" by comparison to the future joy of restored relationship!

---

4   His ultimate goal is summarized in Hebrews 10:7, "I have come to do your will, my God."

5   Luke 14:26.

I know Good Friday (which happens to be tomorrow) typically is a time of solemn reflection. But right now, I feel like I'm sharing Christ's joy, and I just can't stop smiling.

Chapter 20

Reality Therapy
Sovereignty and Subjectivity

King David was a Renaissance man before the term ever existed. He excelled in music, dance, poetry, martial arts, military strategy, leadership, governance, diplomacy, acquiring wives (and fathering children), and of course spirituality.

We probably should add "drama" to the list because he successfully feigned insanity. To escape from Saul's attempt to kill him, David once sought refuge with a Philistine king. But when court officials pointed out the threat he represented, David knew his life was in jeopardy, so "he acted like a madman, making marks on the doors of the gate and letting saliva run down his beard."[1]

It wasn't his finest hour, but it saved his life—and he ended up writing Psalm 34 from that experience, so it wasn't wasted.

But there was another key role David played. In Acts chapter 2 the apostle Peter identifies him as a prophet, which makes sense

---

1   1 Samuel 21:10-15.

considering that the Psalms he wrote included key prophecies about the coming Messiah.

David arguably was the most important prophet of his time. Yet when God wanted to give significant direction to David, he usually spoke to him through *another* prophet. It was Nathan who brought God's word concerning the building of the temple and who courageously confronted David about his sin with Bathsheba.

Why did God do that? If David was both king and prophet, and a man after God's own heart, why didn't God just speak directly to him? David was divinely inspired to write Scriptures like Psalm 23 ("The Lord is my shepherd") and other Psalms quoted by Jesus and the apostles in the New Testament. So why would God use a third party—a "lesser" prophet like Nathan—for some key communication with him?

I can think of three reasons.

First, there's always a danger of pride and arrogance when we think we can hear God for ourselves without reference to anyone else. David could have reasoned, "I have a direct line to God. Why would I need a second-rate prophet like Nathan telling me what God is saying?" Instead, David humbled himself and received Nathan's input for what it was: God's word through God's choice of messenger.

Another reason God may speak through someone else is to avoid subjectivity, especially in matters of great importance to us. As a rule, the more we're invested emotionally in a particular outcome, the more susceptible we are to subjectivity, and the more we need an objective voice—an outside perspective—to ensure we're hearing God correctly.

Thirdly, while God's plan does include direct, personal communication, he also wants to speak and work with us in the context of community and accountability.

And what does that mean? Well, according to the Bible, it's more than just sharing with others about the positives in our lives. We're to share the negatives, too, not in a reality-TV-show kind of way but by being real in our interactions.

And how real does it get? Here's one Scripture that gives us a clue: "Therefore confess your sins to each other and pray for each other so that you may be healed."[2]

Community and accountability are more than nice concepts. They represent God's sovereign plan for the way we are to live. And they challenge us to the core in our attempts to live independent lives, free from the discomfort of honest interaction or the embarrassment of being known as we really are. Even our healing can be at stake.

I've long believed in accountability and mentoring relationships, and I regard integrity—the alignment between what we believe and what we do—as a core value. Good beliefs; good values. Except that on the day I was writing this chapter I came to the unpleasant conclusion that I was personally avoiding accountability!

After wrestling with my thoughts for a while, a few things became clear: I realized I had convinced myself that I could ultimately work out my "issues" without sharing my weaknesses with my pastor—and in any case (I reasoned), he didn't need more problems to think about.

In the end, I had to acknowledge that my choice not to discuss my weaknesses was based on pride and independence, and so, somewhat reluctantly, I changed my mind and decided to have an honest talk at the earliest opportunity. (Changing one's mind and direction is called "repentance" in the Bible.)

God wants us to move beyond guilt and subjectivity and into a place of peace and clarity. Here's how the apostle John puts it:

---

2   James 5:16.

God is light; in him there is no darkness at all. If we claim to have fellowship with him and yet walk in the darkness, we lie and do not live out the truth. But if we walk in the light, as he is in the light, we have fellowship with one another, and the blood of Jesus, his Son, purifies us from all sin.[3]

Who would have thought that God's sovereignty would involve interacting with *people* to such an extent?

Whether it's ordinary people like you or me, or "rock stars" like King David, we're called to move beyond subjectivity through confession and humbly hearing God's voice through the people he sends our way.

---

3   1 John 1:5-7.

Chapter 21

What Cancer Cannot Steal
God's Sovereignty as a Win-Win

It's August 10th. Our 40th wedding anniversary—or it would be if my wife hadn't died ten months earlier. Instead, I'm standing at a grocery checkout counter buying a bouquet of flowers to place on her grave.

The guy in the line-up behind me grins and says, "Oh, you must have been *really* bad, but I'm sure she'll like the flowers."

For a moment I'm tempted to tell him where I'm taking the bouquet, but then decide that it would be cruel to someone who was only trying to be friendly, so I just smile in return.

Sure, the guy was insensitive, but there were more important things going on—like something God had shown me earlier that morning. It was a Scripture I'd read many times before, but this time the words of the apostle Paul took on new meaning: "For to me to live is Christ and to die is gain."[1]

---

1   Philippians 1:21.

What I sensed the Lord saying was simple and straightforward: On this day, the day we would have celebrated 40 years together, I could choose to focus on my loss or on Margarete's gain.

It was exactly what I needed to hear.

Yes, there still was a rightful place for grieving the loss of my beloved wife, but I didn't have to get caught up in depression or self-pity as if it was all about me. Instead, I could thank God for the wonderful person who had been my wife for almost four decades—someone who had lived her life for the Lord and the people around her—and that she had gained her reward.

What exactly had she gained? In one of his letters to the churches, Paul considers the pros and cons of living and dying:

> If I am to go on living in the body, this will mean fruitful labor for me. Yet what shall I choose? I do not know! I am torn between the two: I desire to depart and be with Christ, which is better by far; but it is more necessary for you that I remain in the body.[2]

Countless books have been written and movies made about the life hereafter, but we actually know very little of what it's like. That's not because the Bible is cagey on the subject of heaven, but because eternal life represents another dimension. (Think of a rockfish living its life on the ocean floor, trying to comprehend life above the water.)

But one thing is clear from this Scripture. For Christians, death represents gain: it's life with Christ in a much closer relationship, and it's "better by far" than life on earth. Which means the most idyllic scenario we can imagine on Earth—in terms of beauty, peace,

---

2   Philippians 1:22-24.

joy, pleasure, excitement, creativity, freedom, security, loving rela-tionships—is superseded by the quality of life in heaven.[3]

So, what's the take-away? Simply that God's sovereignty extends over sickness and health, life and death, and *that's* what guarantees a win-win situation for us.

During my wife's battle with cancer, we would write occasional email updates to family and friends. Here's an excerpt from the letter I sent a few months before she passed away:

> *In my email update in December, I said something about ini-tially thinking that everything had changed with the diagnosis of advanced pancreatic cancer, but then realizing that many truly important things had* not *changed. The last time we were at the Cancer Agency in Vancouver I saw a plaque on the wall by an "Author Unknown" who captured these thoughts in a simple yet profound way—as follows:*

Cancer is so limited:
It cannot cripple love
It cannot shatter hope
It cannot corrode faith
It cannot destroy peace
It cannot silence courage
It cannot invade the soul
It cannot steal eternal life
It cannot conquer the spirit

> *I can appreciate the truth of those words on a rational level, but more importantly I can experience the reality of them because of God's goodness and sovereignty and because of your kindness and prayer support. Thank you, and God bless you!*

---

3   For a helpful exploration of the subject, I would recommend *All About Heaven* by David Oliver (Malcolm Down Publishing, UK, 2019).

I'm still amazed at how real God's grace was during that time (and ever since). It reminds me of a famous excerpt from Paul's letter to the Romans:

> For I am convinced that neither death nor life, neither angels nor demons, neither the present nor the future, nor any powers, neither height nor depth, nor anything else in all creation, will be able to separate us from the love of God that is in Christ Jesus our Lord.[4]

That's an eternal truth worth holding on to. It's the ultimate win-win!

---

4   Romans 8:38-39.

Chapter 22

The Heart Has Its Reasons
Sovereign Surprises

"Are you ready for a surprise?"

It was a question that itself came as a surprise—and it was as startling as if I had heard God speak audibly.

I was walking around the Stanley Park seawall, thinking and praying as I often did during those months when my wife was battling cancer, but this took me aback. Was God going to heal Margarete after all this time? That really *would* be a miracle and a wonderful surprise. But if that were his plan, why wouldn't he be a little more direct?

Wondering whether the question I'd heard was rhetorical, I mentally filed it away for future reference and kept on walking.

One thing I definitely did not contemplate was the possibility of marriage after Margarete. In fact, the day after that initial call from the doctor about her cancer diagnosis, I concluded that if God took her, it would mean that he intended for me to live alone.

It all made sense (in a brutal sort of way). Having just retired, I was freed from the constraints of my career. Now, perhaps, I was to be freed from the constraints of marriage in order to focus on writing, ensconced in solitary splendor in my Vancouver West End apartment.

In my befuddled state of mind, I even drew comparisons with the apostle Paul who did much of his writing from prison. My prison would be nicer, of course, but I would be cut off from much of my former social involvement, and I'd just quietly toil away in my cage (gilded though it might be).

So I told Margarete that if the Lord did take her, I intended to stay single the rest of my life. Her reply was not what I expected. She simply said, "That's sweet of you." I didn't know what else to say, so I left it there, and we never returned to the subject. In retrospect, it probably was her way of saying, "I rather doubt it, but I appreciate the thought."

In the year after Margarete's passing, I began corresponding with a long-time friend of hers in Ontario named Dianne—someone we had known from our church when she lived in BC, and who also was single again.

It started very simply: I had not been able to attend her son's wedding, and she had not been able to attend Margarete's memorial service, so we exchanged links to online videos of those two events and then added a few emailed comments.

For some reason, the emails didn't stop. They were sporadic at first, but then gradually picked up momentum as we discussed various subjects from theology to our families to politics to music and books. I also found I could share aspects of my journey of bereavement, as she had known and loved Margarete as a friend for over 40 years.

A book that Dianne recommended, *The Gospel According to Job* by Mike Mason, became a source of great encouragement during this time—as did another book by the same author, *Champagne for the Soul.*

In the latter, Mason quotes one of the Beatitudes of Christ: "Blessed (or happy) are those who mourn."[1]

Then he poses two key questions, which he answers from his own experience:

> Is it possible for the sad to be happy?…Is happiness compatible with sadness, longing, loneliness, frustration? Oddly, I discovered that the answer is yes. Indeed there can be no real happiness without a full range of all the other human emotions accompanying it.[2]

Meanwhile, the surprise of this new relationship—and the accompanying "range of emotions" was growing, and I couldn't help but think of a famous line by Blaise Pascal, "The heart has its reasons, of which reason knows nothing."

In time, our emails were supplemented by phone calls, and eventually we decided to meet in the summer when she would be in Vancouver to take courses at Regent College.

By the time summer came, we had arranged to meet multiple times, and after a number of those dates we found ourselves blissfully—but *unexpectedly*—engaged.

I had in mind to propose to Dianne later in the year, thinking that she (and others) might think it was all happening too fast. But one evening, while the sun was setting on English Bay and Andrea Bocelli was crooning "Love Me Tender" on my CD player, the true feelings of my heart just tumbled out, and she said "yes"!

To this day, neither of us remembers the exact words spoken, or whether our first kiss happened before or after the proposal.

---

1   Matthew 5:4.

2   Mike Mason, *Champagne for the Soul* (Vancouver: Regent College Publishing, 2007), 35.

Apparently we were lost in la-la land, caught up in the sweet delirium of love.

The Lord must have chuckled to himself when he asked me, "Are you ready for a surprise?" I hadn't a clue. But that didn't stop a sovereign, loving, Heavenly Father from preparing a wonderful surprise for an unsuspecting son.

I wonder what surprises he has in store for you?

Section Two

Sovereignty Touches Everything

"There is not a square inch in the whole domain of human existence over which Christ, who is Sovereign over all, does not cry, 'Mine!'"

—*Abraham Kuyper (1837-1920),*
theologian, journalist, and Prime Minister of the Netherlands

Introduction to Section 2

If God Were Not Sovereign...

Three out of four people in the world today believe in God or in some type of deity.[1]

Roughly half of *that* number are Christian—those who believe in the God of the Bible, One who is both sovereign and personal. Within the other half—that is, those who believe in a deity, but not necessarily the God revealed in the Bible—we find a variety of views, such as:

- God created the universe using the laws of physics and mathematics, and then kept his distance, leaving creation (and humanity) to sort itself out.
- God may be present in creation, but he is unknowable.

---

1   According to Pew Research Center, Buddhists and the non-religious currently make up the remaining quarter of the world's population: https://www.pewresearch.org/fact-tank/2017/04/05/christians-remain-worlds-largest-religious-group-but-they-are-declining-in-europe/ (accessed March 11, 2020).

- God is good, but he's locked in battle with an equally powerful force of evil, and that is why there's so much suffering.
- God is more powerful than evil, but his sovereignty—in terms of what he knows and is able to do—is limited by humanity's choices (free will).

Even among Christians there is disagreement on the subject of God's sovereignty, some focusing on his unlimited power, others emphasizing the free will he bestowed on the human race.

We won't get into that debate here. But in introducing our exploration of how God's sovereignty touches everything, I would like to raise a question: What would it look like if God were *not* sovereign?

Strangely enough, one answer to that question might be found in science fiction movies!

It isn't that sci-fi movies are more godless than other types. It's just that when they imagine the distant future, they'll usually depict a time after humanity has nuked the world, or super-intelligent machines have seized control, or marauding monsters are attacking from outer space—all without a hint of God or divine intervention whatsoever.

In fairness, very few movies include divine intervention. But how the future is imagined—especially when it's depicted as dark, mechanical, and oppressive—gives us a haunting sense of what the absence of God looks like. And why do movie makers see the future in such bleak terms? Probably because of our destructive past.

It would be easy to attribute humanity's violent history to a lack of civilization, but the past century has been one of the bloodiest yet, including several failed attempts at creating a utopia on earth—including the Nazis with their Aryan master-race theories and the communists with their dogma of a classless society at whatever cost.

So far, every attempt to create an earthly paradise has failed miserably, resulting in a dystopia of one kind or another. As history demonstrates and sci-fi predicts, those regimes always exercise power at the expense of freedom, human dignity, compassion, and creativity.

To restate the question: If God isn't really sovereign—if he doesn't know everything and isn't all-powerful—would it make any difference to life on earth, to our personal lives, to our hope for the future? Yes, yes, and yes.

- Without a God who knew all there was to know and who shared knowledge with us, there would be no way of knowing what was true. Everything would be a matter of opinion, the perspective of fallible beings who could grasp only a limited portion of reality.
- If God didn't know everything that was coming and lacked the power to ensure it turned out "right," there could be no solid hope for the future.
- We would have no assurance of our sins being forgiven if God could be wrong about the sacrifice of Jesus being sufficient to pay for it all.
- If it were possible for God to be mistaken about his predictions or unable to keep his promises, we couldn't rely on the truth and authority of the Bible.
- There would be no ultimate basis for right and wrong, no ethical foundation on which to base our core values.[2]
- In the absence of an almighty God, we would live in fear of what could happen—someone starting a nuclear war by mistake, a meteor wiping out all life

---

2   Some ethics practitioners would disagree, but that view often avoids the issue of presuppositions.

on Earth, artificial intelligence systems taking control in the future (assuming aliens from outer space didn't subjugate us first!). The list of potential doomsday scenarios is long and fearsome.

The apostle Paul told the Corinthians, "If Christ has not been raised, your faith is futile; you are still in your sins." He goes on to say, "If only for this life we have hope in Christ, we are of all people most to be pitied."[3]

We might well add a parallel statement: *If God is not sovereign*, we are a hopeless and pitiful lot.

The good news is that we do have a God who is sovereign! That's a reality that touches every facet of life on this planet—from ethics and values to spiritual matters; from evil and suffering in this world to life after death; from the most private issues of the heart to the global realm of the nations.

As we explore these facets, I'm hoping we'll find answers to some basic questions:

- What can I learn about God and his point of view on each subject?
- What difference does his sovereignty make, practically speaking?
- If what I'm learning is true, how do I need to change?

The reason we ask such questions is because it's never enough just to get the theory right. The book of James puts it rather bluntly: "You believe that there is one God. Good! Even the demons believe that—and shudder."[4] In other words, what we believe isn't of much use if it doesn't affect what we say and do.

---

3   1 Corinthians 15:17,19.

4   James 2:19.

This section will include material that may seem a bit technical at times, but it's all intended to help us interact with the reality of a sovereign God who doesn't want to be just "believed in" at arm's length, but also loved, trusted, and obeyed.

My hope is that we'll get beyond the theology and principles involved and (re)discover the Person we're dealing with. Based on my own experience, I know he will prove to be reassuring where we have needlessly worried and challenging where we have acted presumptuously.

I've often been encouraged by how patiently Jesus taught his disciples. He took the time needed to deconstruct their faulty worldview, challenge their wrong assumptions, and show them the way, the truth, and the life.[5] He will do the same for us as we listen for his voice and embrace our role as lifelong learners (that is, disciples).

Since we're dealing with a God who is infinite, I fully expect the learning process to continue in eternity. For now, though, we focus on acknowledging his sovereignty in every realm where it applies—which happens to be *everywhere, everyone,* and *everything.* No exceptions.

---

5   John 14:6.

Chapter 23

No Limits
Sovereignty and Infinity

When I tried googling "No Limits" this morning, I found all manner of goods and services using that name. There were *No Limits* fitness academies, motivational books, banking services, T-shirts, auto parts, barbecue sauce, hot yoga, and even churches.

That may seem like a list of totally unrelated things, but I can assure you they have one thing in common. Regardless of the name, they all have limits!

So, why are we attracted to the idea of no limits? Is it egotism? Rebellion? Delusions of grandeur?

Those may all be part of the equation, but there's a more universal element to consider. Scripture tells us that God has "set eternity in the human heart."[1]

In some strange way, we're able to imagine the concept of eternity—or infinity—even if we can't fully comprehend it. And so we throw around terms like *ultimate, absolute, supreme,* and *no limits,*

---

1   Ecclesiastes 3:11.

all of which (if we're being accurate) could never apply to anyone or anything besides the Sovereign God we read about in the Bible.

Here's one description from the Psalms: "Great is our Lord and mighty in power; / his understanding has *no limit*," and, "his greatness no one can fathom."[2]

Have you ever thought about the fact that God knows absolutely everything? Humanity has developed an amazing knowledge base and can mobilize supercomputers to estimate the answers to many questions, but God knows the *precise* answer to any and all questions.

For example…

The Milky Way galaxy in which our planet and solar system reside contains between 100 billion and 400 billion stars, and the universe contains about 2 trillion *galaxies*. Those are our best estimates.[3] But God knows the number precisely: "He determines the number of the stars / and calls them each by name."[4]

Numbers in the billions and trillions are not easy to grasp, so a simple illustration may help. How long would it take to go through a billion dollars if you spent a dollar per minute? Hint: Start with the fact that there are 1,440 minutes in a 24-hour day, which would equal $1,440 per day.

If you continued that rate of spending seven days/week, 365 days/year, it would take you over 1,900 years to spend that $1 billion. It's a big number. And spending a trillion would take you more than 1,900,000 years.

That brings us to the question: Why would God create such a vast universe?

---

2   Psalm 147:5 and 145:3 (emphasis added).

3   https://www.nationalgeographic.com/science/space/universe/galaxies/ (Accessed September 30, 2020).

4   Psalm 147:4.

The simplest answer is: Why not? If you're the Creator with no limits, why *not* make it big? It's not as if an infinite Creator ever runs out of resources or power or time.

Then, as we think about the massive size of the universe, we may wonder whether there's life anywhere besides Earth.

The simplest answer: nobody knows. If God decided to create life elsewhere, that would be his prerogative. But the sheer size of the universe has nothing to do with it. For a Creator with unlimited wisdom and power to make a universe with life on just one planet is a non-issue. Even if our universe were one of many (as a few scientists like to speculate), again, that's not an issue for a Creator with no limits.

The advancement of scientific knowledge in the 21ˢᵗ century has not only expanded our understanding of the universe, it also has forced a rethinking of the role of a Creator.

One reason for that is "fine-tuning." Just as a car engine needs to be tuned by carefully designing its parts to function within certain tolerances, the universe as a whole and the earth in particular also need to be fine-tuned in order for advanced life to exist—to an extent that is almost unimaginably precise.

Astronomer Hugh Ross lists 150 different parameters for which a planet, its moon, its star, and its galaxy must have values falling within narrow ranges in order for life of *any* kind to exist.[5] For the universe as a whole, the degree of fine-tuning is mind-numbing—especially when it comes to dark energy, which makes up about 68% of the universe.[6] Here's how Dr. Ross describes it:

> If one were to compare the fine-tuning design of dark energy to make advanced life possible with the best example

---

5   Hugh Ross, *The Creator and the Cosmos*, fourth edition (Covina, California: Reasons to Believe, 2018), Appendix B, 243-266.

6   https://science.nasa.gov/astrophysics/focus-areas/what-is-dark-energy.

of fine-tuning design achieved by humans, the design of dark energy would rank about 10^{99} times superior, that is, superior by a factor of one thousand trillion trillion trillion trillion trillion trillion trillion trillion times.

What does this superior fine-tuning design say about the One who created the universe? It implies that at a minimum this One is 10^{99} times more intelligent and more knowledgeable than the most brilliant scientists and engineers.[7]

For comparative purposes, scientists estimate the total number of atoms in the entire universe as 10^{80}. So perhaps it's easier just to say that God is *infinitely* greater than his creatures!

Which means that when the Bible says, "The heavens declare the glory of God,"[8] it's the pinnacle of understatement.

Our Creator really is the ultimate in knowledge, wisdom, power, and creativity.

He's the God of no limits.

---

7   Ross, *Creator and the Cosmos,* 54-55. Further background on Dr. Hugh Ross and his think tank on faith and science called "Reasons to Believe" can be found at www.reasons.org.

8   Psalm 19:1.

Chapter 24

A Fine-Tuned You
Sovereignty and DNA

One-year-olds generally are known for their messiness, happily smearing food wherever they can reach. But here was our baby daughter in a highchair, holding up her hands and making "protesting" sounds, all because her little fingers had become sticky.

I was aware that I *myself* hated sticky fingers, but after witnessing our one-year-old's reaction and remembering that my father also seemed to dislike stickiness, I asked him if either of his parents were that way. Sure enough: apparently it came from his mother.

Of course, my wife and I had a good laugh. An "aversion-to-stickiness" gene? How weird is that?

A closer look at the wonders of genetics reveals how weird and wonderful it actually is—and the astounding genetic complexity involved.

You may recall from science class that our DNA contains all of the information needed to build and maintain every part of our body, which takes more than 3 billion DNA base pairs in the nucleus of our cells.

And the size of the human cell? Well, it would take about 10,000 of them to cover the head of a pin.

Because of DNA's capacity to store massive amounts of complex information in a microscopic space, computer scientists are now actively seeking ways of using these molecules to store data.

A principal researcher at Microsoft, Karen Strauss, puts it this way: "Think of compressing all the information on the accessible Internet into a shoebox. With DNA data storage, that's possible."[1]

At the risk of making your head spin, I will add some statistics that relate to how each of us came to be who we are. We'll start with the fact that there are slight differences in the genetic blueprint of each egg and each sperm cell, and that the numbers involved are enormous—women being born with about two million eggs and men producing hundreds of billions of sperm over a lifetime.

Those numbers of reproductive cells are greatly reduced if we count only those involved during childbearing years. But even taking a very conservative estimate of just a three-year period in which a couple may be trying to have children, the possible combinations of eggs and sperm during that time are approximately 12 trillion![2]

Faced with those mind-boggling numbers, we have two choices: we can believe it's all down to chance, or we can believe we are who we are because God chose to make a certain person with a unique set of characteristics. The implications of these two viewpoints are very different.

---

1   https://www.forbes.com/sites/johncumbers/2019/08/03/dna-data-storage-is-about-to-go-viral/#224d32877721.

2   In addition, there is a factor called *mosaicism*—mutations that randomly form different patterns in different people, such that the same zygote would never develop exactly the same way twice—per https://www.nytimes.com/2018/05/21/science/mosaicism-dna-genome-cancer.html.

Are my characteristics—my height, my IQ, my voice, my hair, my facial structure, my strengths and weaknesses, my quirks—just the product of chance, or did God deliberately make the choice to create me the way he did?

There are several good reasons to believe we're here by his choice, not chance:

- For a truly infinite God, choosing from trillions of possible genetic combinations (and maybe adding a few interesting mutations) is not a problem. With him there's no limitation of knowledge, wisdom, time, creativity, purpose, or anything else.

- Given the evidence of God's fine-tuning of the inanimate parts of creation, wouldn't he exercise at least the same degree of fine-tuning in creating the only beings made in his own image?

- God sent his only Son to die so that we could live with him eternally. By that measure the value he places on us is incalculable, which makes it reasonable to conclude he also gave great care and attention to our design.

- The Bible tells us that God "chose us in him [Jesus Christ] before the creation of the world to be holy and blameless in his sight."[3] In other words, he knew exactly who he was going to create even before the earth came into being!

Here is how the Psalmist describes it:
For you created my inmost being;
you knit me together in my mother's womb.
I praise you because I am fearfully and wonderfully made…[4]

---

3   Ephesians 1:4.

4   Psalm 139:13-14.

If we think about what these realities mean for our lives, what should we conclude? If God sovereignly chose to create you and me and everyone else according to a detailed, divine plan, what does that mean in practice?

It means we need to fully accept how God created us—the specific characteristics we were born with as well as our family lineage and racial background.

It also means we need to regard everyone as having great value, dignity, and purpose. We may disagree with what people do, but to put them down—to denigrate their inborn characteristics—is to directly insult their Creator.[5]

The final word goes to the Psalmist in this beautifully profound image of how God created us:

> My frame was not hidden from you
>> when I was made in the secret place,
>> when I was woven together in the depths of
> the earth.
> Your eyes saw my unformed body;
>> all the days ordained for me were written in
> your book
>> before one of them came to be.[6]

---

5   An obvious example of that would be racially motivated mistreatment.

6   Psalm 139:15-16.

Chapter 25

Coincidence, Control, or Chance?
Sovereignty and Probability (Part 1)

You've probably heard people say, "God is in control." Maybe you've used that phrase yourself. If so, what do you think God's control includes?

A devastating hurricane? Even agnostic insurance brokers refer to that as an act of God.

A car accident? What if the other driver was drunk, or there was a mechanical failure?

A bad roll of the dice when you're playing Snakes and Ladders? Well, that sounds too trivial, doesn't it? But then, where exactly is the line between what's too trivial and what's important enough for God to control?

I'll never forget the first time I saw the Probability Machine at the Pacific Science Center in Seattle—a large rectangular exhibit enclosed by plexiglass revealing evenly spaced metal pegs inside (almost like a giant pinball machine standing on end) with small compartments at the bottom. A chain drive would slowly bring colorful plastic balls to the top-center and then drop them.

Through the plexiglass you would see balls bounce randomly among the pegs on their way down to the compartments below. Here's what I found fascinating: While there was no way of predicting where any individual ball would end up, the majority landed in the middle sections and progressively fewer at the sides. After the cycle was done, the pattern displayed by the number of balls in each compartment was the famous bell curve, visually demonstrating the principle of probability.

So—a few questions in relation to God's sovereignty:

Did God create probability? Of course. He created everything.

Does he know where each ball will end up every time the Probability Machine runs? Of course. He knows everything. Just because some information seems unimportant doesn't mean God doesn't know it. Volume of information is a non-issue for an infinite God. There's no "overload" factor.

Does God *control* where each ball ends up? Ah, that's where it gets interesting. Answering this seemingly minor question raises some very different views on sovereignty.

Some people believe in the existence of a Creator, but that such a being simply created the laws of physics (including probability), started the universe, and then let it run its course—a hands-off approach.

At the other end of the spectrum are those who believe God's sovereignty involves *direct* control of every detail, regardless of humanity's free will or the actions of other entities like angels and demons—a deterministic model with a completely hands-on Creator.

Still others, trying to reconcile the goodness of God with the fact of evil in this world, propose the idea of "limited sovereignty" so that God can't be blamed for everything that goes wrong. Or they emphasize the difference between what God does directly and what he *allows* to happen.

Leaving aside the wide range of opinion on the subject, we can safely say that the Bible shows God to be hands-on in his dealings with people, and yet he created us with free will; we're not robots. That means he doesn't initiate every action that takes place, and some things he allows on earth are obviously contrary to his standards and values. And yet his sovereignty is absolute.[1]

I'm reminded of the paradox of the nature of Jesus Christ—according to what the Bible teaches and what the Church has affirmed for the past 2,000 years: that he is fully God and fully human.

Our minds may insist he cannot be fully both: that there must be some percentage of God and humanity—whether 50/50 or 60/40 or whatever—which combined would add up to 100%. But that's not Scripture, and so we must accept the reality of his nature as an article of faith.

Some would argue that involving faith is irrational. But then, is it logical to think our puny minds could grasp the true nature of the incarnation—God becoming a man: infinity in finite form?

By the same token, shouldn't we *expect* to encounter aspects of God's sovereignty we cannot fully grasp, especially as we hold onto truths that seem to be in tension?[2]

A final point: Hands-on sovereignty doesn't necessarily mean direct involvement. We find instances in the Bible where an intermediary—for example, an angel—brings God's message to someone on earth.

Does God's use of an intermediary diminish his sovereignty? Of course not. Neither would the use of an intermediary in the form

---

1   The question of how humanity's free will and God's sovereignty coexist is an important subject and will be the focus of another chapter.

2   While such a comment could be regarded as a cop-out, there is no avoiding the existence of paradoxes in Scripture (nor, for that matter, in the natural world, as even a cursory look at quantum mechanics will demonstrate).

of God's laws of physics, mathematics, chemistry, or biology detract from his sovereignty.

In truth, we don't actually know the degree to which God involves himself directly in the minutiae of life. From what we've learned about fine-tuning, one could argue he's probably more involved than we think.

But whether God exercises his sovereignty directly or indirectly, he still is in charge. We need never doubt the range of his knowledge, nor the reach of his power, nor the scope of his ultimate reign. As the Psalmist says of the Creator, "*All* things serve you."[3]

---

3   Psalm 119:91 (emphasis added)

Chapter 26

Luck of the Draw
Sovereignty and Probability (Part 2)

People in the ancient world would often cast lots in order to settle disputes or answer questions. They might use several white pebbles with one black one or little sticks with one shorter one, or sometimes pieces of bone.[1] A modern day equivalent would be flipping a coin or throwing dice.

One of the Proverbs states, "The lot is cast into the lap, / but its every decision is from the Lord."[2] How are we to understand that? Is it a blanket statement that covers everything we might otherwise call *chance*? And how does it relate to the laws of probability?

These are not just theoretical questions pertaining to science and theology. They can affect us in very personal and practical ways. An embarrassing story comes to mind, by way of illustration.

---

1   The Israelites even had mysterious but God-sanctioned devices called the *Urim and Thummim*, which were linked to the breastplate of the high priest.

2   Proverbs 16:33.

I was about 21 years old and had experienced a spiritual renewal that made me more open to the Holy Spirit and less dependent on intellectual reasoning. As a way of hearing God through Scripture, I had devised a little system that I thought would minimize my personal bias in the process. It involved putting numbered pieces of paper in a bag representing the 150 Psalms and the 31 Proverbs. Then, whenever I wanted to hear God, I would simply pull one out, and *presto!*

The experiment ended badly.

I had been asked to emcee a friend's wedding reception and to read a Scripture as part of the program. Thinking I was being extra spiritual by not preparing the Scripture in advance, I pulled the number of a Psalm from the bag before the program, and then read it out without having checked it first.

It was one of *those* Psalms—the ones theologians call imprecatory Psalms—where it's asking God to slay the wicked and exact vengeance on his enemies. I persevered to the end of the reading, my face burning as I knew the wedding guests would be totally mystified by my choice of Scripture.

The good news: the wedding survived my faux pas (as did the marriage). And I was cured from relying on a type of "Bible Bingo" for guidance.

In retrospect, I believe God knew exactly what was going to happen. He could have led me to an appropriate Psalm for the occasion, but he knew it was an opportunity for me to learn an important lesson.

And lessons—or learning opportunities—are critical in our maturing. This is a lifelong process, and the methods God uses often involve other people or even inanimate objects that appear to function by chance or probability.

As long as I can remember, I've been one of those drivers who chafes at slow traffic and everything else that impedes efficient movement on the road. When we moved to the West End of Vancouver—apparently the most densely populated neighborhood in Canada and where traffic moves at a snail's pace—it turned out to be a perfect learning opportunity.

I certainly can't claim a personality make-over, but my attitude and my driving did gradually change as I chose to view other cars and even traffic signals not as human-controlled impediments but as instruments that God was using to teach me patience. (It's a work in progress, as my wife could confirm!)[3]

If I were unwilling to recognize God's sovereignty in a practical situation like traffic, I could be stuck in a scenario where I might be listening to a hymn like *This is My Father's World* and agreeing with the words, but all the while fuming at the people and circumstances on the road as if they were *outside* God's world, that is, outside his control.

There is a famous quote, sometimes attributed to Einstein, which says, "There are only two ways to live your life. One is as though nothing is a miracle. The other is as though everything is."

I'd like to appropriate that idea by stating it another way: We can live as though God is absent from everything in our lives, or as though he is present in every circumstance and situation.

When we believe he is truly present and actively involved, we never have to live in fear or superstition, we don't need to worry about conspiracy theories, and we never have to feel we're the victim of circumstance or bad luck.

---

3   Evidently I am not alone in being "traffic-challenged." One commentator offered this summary of our sometimes-jaundiced viewpoint: "Everyone driving slower than you is a turkey, and everyone driving faster than you is an idiot."

Even without a perfect understanding of how God directs what we call chance, luck, or probability, trusting in his sovereignty is the crucial path to peace, maturity, wisdom, and grace.

You can bet on it!

Chapter 27

A One-Owner World
Sovereignty and Ownership (Part 1)

Have you ever heard the phrase, "Possession is nine-tenths of the law"?

It's an idea that's been around for hundreds of years, and simply means that if you've got something in your possession, it's generally presumed to belong to you unless someone can prove otherwise. And proving otherwise can take a long time—as when disputes about "who owns what" end up in court.[1]

Ownership isn't always obvious. People renting a house may look and function the same as homeowners in their use of a property. But the status quo can change promptly if the homeowners decide to occupy the property themselves.

---

1   For example, in British Columbia, Canada, where I live, overlapping land claims by Indigenous peoples cover over 100% of the province, while uncertainty grows regarding who has a legal, moral, and historic right to the land, given past injustices and unresolved treaty negotiations.

And ownership does not necessarily mean effective control—at least not in the short term. That certainly became obvious as we were subject to lockdowns during the COVID-19 pandemic.

You could try claiming that beaches and parks are public property and that as a citizen of a town, city, province, state, or country, you are part-owner of those public lands and have the right to use them. But you would soon discover that ownership does not equal control.

Actual control in this case is in the hands of the leaders we elect and the officials they hire. Yes, we (collectively speaking) can replace politicians in order to change laws and regulations, but the process of doing so takes time and effort (and often a lot of money), and even then, the outcome is far from certain.

The point is that ownership, occupancy, and control are related, but they don't necessarily operate together at a particular point in time. That's very important to keep in mind as we look at how God's ownership functions.

There's something else to keep in mind: the question of what we really mean by the word ownership. In the Western world we have constitutions, bills of rights, and common law (established legal precedents) that form the basis of what we call private property rights.

The recognition of private property is the foundation of many other rights, so its value should not be underrated. And yet even in the most democratic of countries we find legal loopholes such as *eminent domain*, also known as *compulsory purchase* and *expropriation*.

That's when the government decides your property is exactly where they need to build a road or a park or a pipeline. And because the "common good" is more important than your property rights, they can legally take your land in exchange for an amount they consider just compensation.

So, you can be the lawful owner of a piece of property (a man's home is his castle, as the saying goes), and yet the government seems to consider itself the ultimate owner and you, effectively, a leaseholder.

Even though these powers may not be used very often, they show us that property ownership is far from absolute. And even governments' ownership powers can be overturned during wartime or the rise and fall of empires.

There is, in fact, only one Person whose ownership status is absolute and not subject to dispute, seizure, negotiation, or limitation—God Almighty, Creator of heaven and earth.

As Moses put it to the Israelites: "To the Lord your God belong the heavens, even the highest heavens, the earth and everything in it...For the Lord your God is God of gods and Lord of lords, the great God, mighty and awesome..."[2]

God expresses it in very concrete terms to the Israelites—who were trying to impress him with sacrifices in the way that their pagan neighbors tried to gain favor with their gods:

I have no need of a bull from your stall
    or of goats from your pens,
for every animal of the forest is mine,
    and the cattle on a thousand hills.
I know every bird in the mountains
    and the insects in the fields are mine.
If I were hungry I would not tell you,
    for the world is mine, and all that is in it.[3]

Job was one of the great men of faith in the Bible, but during his suffering he complained about not getting the hearing he felt God owed him. Here is part of God's response:

Who has a claim against me that I must pay?

---

2   Deuteronomy 10:14, 17.

3   Psalm 50:9-12.

Everything under heaven belongs to me.[4]

"Everything under heaven." Well, that would include land, sea, plants, animals, countries, cities, houses, cars, money, stock markets, universities, factories, airlines, ships, crops, oil and gas, books, electronic devices, and the Internet.

And everything else. Including *us*, as the Psalmist points out:

The earth is the Lord's, and everything in it,

the world, and all who live in it.[5]

We will look further at the ownership of "all who live in it" in upcoming chapters. For now, may I suggest taking time to reflect on these all-encompassing claims of God—and think about what it means to live in a One-Owner world.

---

4   Job 41:11.

5   Psalm 24:1.

Chapter 28

All Creatures Great and Small
Sovereignty and Ownership (Part 2)

Ownership has always been linked to rights, whether the subject is slavery, abortion, or even the status of animals.

In 2018, members of the Nonhuman Rights Project tried to establish "legal personhood" for two chimpanzees in the New York Court of Appeal, challenging the idea that such animals could be "owned."[1]

In another legal battle, People for the Ethical Treatment of Animals (PETA) sought to convince the courts that animals—in this case, a macaque which had managed to take a selfie—should have the right to own copyrights.[2]

---

1   https://www.nytimes.com/2018/04/07/opinion/sunday/chimps-legal-personhood.html.

2   There was an out-of-court settlement in this case (https://www.npr.org/sections/thetwo-way/2017/09/12/550417823/-animal-rights-advocates-photographer-compromise-over-ownership-of-monkey-selfie).

Meanwhile, PETA has been campaigning to replace the word *pet* with something like *companion* or *human carer*. According to a spokesperson, "A lot of people at home who have dogs or cats will call them pets and refer to themselves as owners and this implies that the animals are a possession, like a car for example."[3]

PETA may represent a minority viewpoint, but at least they're taking their argument to its logical conclusion: that if animals have inherent rights, we cannot call ourselves their owners.

On the strictly human side of the ownership/rights issue, we could point to the historic battle in which slave owners, intent on holding on to their "property rights," fought against those who insisted that no one, regardless of race or color, should ever be treated as property.

More recently, battles have been fought over abortion, with both sides seeing it as a rights issue. One side says a fetus is just part of a woman's body and that therefore she should have the ownership rights to do with "it" as she pleases.[4]

For the other side, each fetus is a pre-born baby that should have a right to life like any other human being, and no one should presume to own him or her, except in the sense of children "belonging" to their parents—a sense that obviously excludes the right to harm them.

One of the Bible's clearest statements on the ownership of people is when Ezekiel quotes God as saying, "For everyone belongs to me, the parent as well as the child—both alike belong to me."[5]

While the U.S. Declaration of Independence is not on par with Scripture, it also speaks powerfully to this issue:

---

3   https://www.foxnews.com/lifestyle/
peta-mocked-pet-derogatory-term-companion.

4   Of course, this ignores the biological fact that a fetus is genetically different from his/her mother.

5   Ezekiel 18:4.

> We hold these truths to be self-evident, that all men are created equal, that they are endowed by their Creator with certain unalienable Rights, that among these are Life, Liberty and the pursuit of Happiness.[6]

The framers of the *Declaration* may not have understood "created equal" as applying equally to women and African Americans, but they were on target in this: that human rights have their foundation in our creation.

They insisted that these "unalienable rights" come from God, that they're not gifts from government, and that they're not just the product of our own efforts. It was a radical idea in 1776, and it remains so in the 21st century as statism, humanism, and other *isms* seem as entrenched as ever.

Exactly what difference does it make that God created us? And how does this apply in a world of genetic manipulation and "designer babies"?

Someone might argue that genetic engineering means a human being, rather than God, decides on the new life that's created. There's no question that people can have a significant influence on life—but only within the framework that God allows.

To take an extreme example, consider the life of a baby that's born because of rape. If we say the baby's *design* is wrong because of the evil act of his or her father, we deny God's sovereignty.

A related online search yielded dozens of heart-warming stories of men and women who had been conceived in rape, yet were leading fulfilling lives despite their difficult start in life. One of them, Rebecca Kiessling, wrote:

---

6   https://www.ushistory.org/declaration/document/.

The rapist is not my creator, as some people would have me believe. My value and identity are not established as a "product of rape," but a child of God. [7]

As they have done throughout history, people assert ownership over lands, resources, ideas, artistic creations, plants, animals, and people. Sometimes they base their claims on legal arguments; other times, it's just "might makes right."

But none can compare to God's ownership claims—based on his creation of our space-time universe, his formation of each and every human being, his direct intervention in our world through Jesus Christ, and his sovereign involvement in the totality of life.

He owns us—but he doesn't treat us like anything else in all creation. As the prophet Malachi describes it, those who fear the Lord and honor his name are treated as children of a loving Father.

We are called his *"treasured* possession."[8]

---

7   https://thelifeinstitute.net/learning-centre/abortion-effects/children/ conceived-in-rape.

8   Malachi 3:16-17 (emphasis added).

Chapter 29

My Choice or God's Will?
Sovereignty, Free Will, and Election

For most of us, elections aren't rare events, and yet voting never quite loses its novelty and awkwardness. We muddle through the forms and then, using a pencil or an electronic button or lever, choose the preferred candidate(s) and slowly walk away, hoping we've avoided any procedural mistakes—or bad choices.

God also gets involved in choosing people in a process he calls "election."

Jesus, Peter, and Paul all mention "the elect" when referring to God's people. A section in one of Peter's letters includes these sweeping statements:

> His divine power has given us everything we need for a godly life through our knowledge of him who called us by his own glory and goodness.
> Therefore, my brothers and sisters, make every effort to confirm your calling and election.[1]

---

1   2 Peter 1:3,10.

If you're a Christian, it means that at some point you chose (or elected) Jesus Christ as Lord and Savior, whether it was a sudden decision or a series of steps over time.

But there's more to it. Scripture tells us it wouldn't have happened if God hadn't first called and elected *you.*

Of course, God's "vote" isn't the same as our democratic system of casting a ballot, and he's never nervous about making mistakes. But it's still a deliberate choice.

Members of Reformed churches will recognize this as territory that John Calvin staked out in the 16th century. For Calvin, *election, calling,* and *predestination* were key tenets of God's sovereignty— which happens to be true, even if we may not agree with every Calvinist doctrine.

Here is how the Scriptures summarize it:

> Praise be to the God and Father of our Lord Jesus Christ…
> For he chose us in him before the creation of the world to be holy and blameless in his sight. In love he predestined us for adoption to sonship through Jesus Christ, in accordance with his pleasure and will…
> In him we were also chosen, having been predestined according to the plan of him who works out everything in conformity with the purpose of his will.[2]

It doesn't take a degree in theology to recognize that these verses highlight God's sovereignty: *he* makes the first move ("he chose us in him before the creation of the world"), *he* predestines us according to his plan, and ultimately *he* works out everything to line up with his will.

That's fine as far as God's side is concerned. But where does that leave room for human will? Are we simply *destined* to be good or

---

2   Ephesians 1:3-5,11.

bad? Is God arbitrary in choosing one person and not another? Is free will an illusion?

Those might be our conclusions if we read only certain verses in the Bible. But other Scriptures emphasize the active choices *we* make—such as listening to God, coming to Jesus, calling on his name, repenting, choosing to serve him, and doing his will:

- "Hear me, my people, and I will warn you—if you would only listen to me, Israel!"[3]
- "Come to me, all you who are weary and burdened, and I will give you rest."[4]
- "Everyone who calls on the name of the Lord will be saved."[5]
- "In the past God overlooked such ignorance, but now he commands all people everywhere to repent."[6]
- "Choose for yourselves this day whom you will serve…"[7]
- "Anyone who chooses to do the will of God will find out whether my teaching comes from God or whether I speak on my own."[8]

So, does the Bible teach that God is completely sovereign *and* that we have free will? That God predestines us, but that we still choose?

Yes and yes.

---

3   Psalm 81:8. See also verses 11-16 as God expresses his longing for people to choose his ways.

4   Matthew 11:28.

5   Romans 10:13.

6   Acts 17:30.

7   Joshua 24:15.

8   John 7:17.

Nicky Gumbel, who pioneered the *Alpha Course* that currently is running in over 100 countries, puts it this way:

> It is not 50% "predestination" and 50% "free will." Jesus says we are 100% predestined and we have 100% free will. This may seem impossible, but God is able to transcend and yet not distort human freedom. We ultimately see this in the incarnation: Jesus is 100% God and 100% human; he is fully God and fully human.[9]

The word *transcend* is key when we're dealing with an infinite God because sometimes truth transcends our understanding. Not to condone intellectual laziness, but is it reasonable to think we could fully grasp the most profound spiritual realities when we struggle to comprehend the material world around us?[10]

In Christ, God's sovereignty in choosing us—and our free will in choosing him—combine. Jesus said: "All those the Father gives me will come to me, and whoever comes to me I will never drive away."[11]

For the apostle Paul, it's our will and God's will working in unison:

> Continue to work out your salvation with fear and trembling, for it is God who works in you to will and to act in order to fulfill his good purpose.[12]

I may not fully understand how it all works, but I know it's 100% good news: "election results" worth celebrating for time and eternity!

------

9   Nicky Gumbel, "Just Relax and Let God Be God," *Bible in One Year, Alpha International*, January 14, 2019, http://www.bibleinoneyear.org/bioy/commentary/3550.

10 In physics, for example, scientists grapple with the paradox of light (photons) being understood as both particles and waves.

11 John 6:37.

12 Philippians 2:12-13.

Chapter 30

Smite Makes Right?
Sovereignty, Justice, and Judgment (Part 1)

One of Gary Larson's famous *Far Side* cartoons imagines God at his computer. On the monitor you see a piano being lowered above an unsuspecting passerby, while God is deciding whether to execute judgment, his finger poised over the keyboard's "SMITE" button.[1]

Do you sometimes wish God used his "SMITE" button on the bad guys? Or wonder why he doesn't get more directly involved in judging evil on this earth?

He could, of course.

You might even have a few targets to recommend for "smiting": child molesters, drug lords, human traffickers, and terrorists. (Just to begin with.)

A sovereign God could use any number of methods to bring instant judgment if he wanted to—including strokes, heart attacks, freak accidents, thunderbolts, and, yes, even falling pianos.

---

1   Gary Larson, *Cows of Our Planet* (Kansas City, Missouri: Andrews and McMeel, 1992), 47.

The Bible does offer a few cases of evildoers being judged directly by God—like King Herod, whose life of pride and cruelty came to a sudden end when "an angel of the Lord struck him down, and he was eaten by worms and died."[2]

But most of the time God delegates the administration of justice to *people*. Or he decides to wait until the last judgment (at the end of human history) to bring a final reckoning.

We may have a problem with either approach. Why, for example, wouldn't God take out a Hitler or a Stalin before they did so much harm? Hitler survived over 30 assassination attempts. Couldn't God have helped at least one of those plots to succeed?[3]

The desire for justice—and the frustration we feel when justice is denied—are both a reflection of our Maker. The prophet Isaiah quotes God as saying, "For I, the Lord, love justice; / I hate robbery and wrongdoing."[4] The Psalmist repeats that theme: "For the Lord is righteous, / he loves justice…" and, "righteousness and justice are the foundation of his throne."[5]

Question: If justice is so important to God, why would he delegate it to human agents—judges, legislators, police officers, soldiers, people like you and me (that is, people who make mistakes)—instead of handling it himself?

If we go as far back as the time of Noah, we find these instructions from God:

> And from each human being, too, I will demand an accounting for the life of another human being.

---

2   Acts 12:23.

3   For a debate on the hypothetical outcome had such a plot succeeded, see https://www.historyextra.com/period/second-world-war/should-we-be-glad-the-plot-to-kill-hitler-failed/.

4   Isaiah 61:8.

5   Psalm 11:7 and 97:2.

> Whoever sheds human blood,
>> by humans shall their blood be shed;
> for in the image of God
>> has God made mankind.[6]

Later instructions in the Bible clarify that administering justice is the task of governments, not individuals, and that Jesus's teaching doesn't allow for revenge. But the command that *people* take responsibility for dispensing justice on earth has never been rescinded. God has never taken back that mandate and begun to use thunderbolts instead.

Which brings us back to the question of why.

Even the best justice systems on earth can fail miserably, freeing the guilty on legal technicalities or mistakenly imprisoning—even executing—the innocent. Whenever people are involved, mistakes will be made.

But God already knew that. When the apostle Paul refers to governing authorities as "God's servants, agents of wrath to bring punishment on the wrongdoer,"[7] he's writing in the context of Roman rule, which was far more arbitrary and corrupt than what most of us are used to.

Paul would have been well aware that the only truly innocent and righteous man in all of history—Jesus Christ—was executed under the Roman justice system. But he also would have understood the following truths:

- Imperfect justice is far better than anarchy.

---

6   Genesis 9:5-6.

7   Romans 13:4.

- Other than Jesus, no one is truly innocent. Ultimately, we cannot claim we deserve fair treatment for ourselves.[8]
- Humans exercising authority and administering justice are key components of the free will God bestowed on mankind.
- Because of God's sovereignty, he is able to work everything—even injustice—for the good.[9]
- The defects of justice dispensed in this life will pale in the light of the punishments and rewards that the Lord will mete out in eternity.
- According to Scripture, God's people are destined to reign with him and even to "judge angels."[10] Dealing with justice issues in this life is part of our training for eternity.

We'll focus on a key problem we have with God's approach to justice—his apparent delay, his *waiting*—in the next chapter. But a closing illustration may help us start thinking about it.

Going back to the *Far Side* example, would you have wanted God to press the "SMITE" button on the nasty slave-traders of the 1700s? If so, you would have taken out John Newton, who became a Christian and in later years helped abolish the slave trade in the British Empire. He also ended up writing one of the best-loved hymns of all time: *Amazing Grace*.

---

8   Psalm 103:10 states that God "does not treat us as our sins deserve or repay us according to our iniquities," suggesting that any injustices we may suffer are still *less* than what we deserve.

9   Romans 8:28.

10   2 Timothy 2:12 and 1 Corinthians 6:3.

Chapter 31

Justice Delayed
Sovereignty, Justice, and Judgment (Part 2)

Besides conquering kings and subduing nearby nations, King David composed poems and wrote songs—we call them *Psalms*—which were then sung by Israel's three major choirs.

The leader of one of those choirs was Asaph, who himself contributed a number of Psalms, one of which was Psalm 73, a brutally honest account of his distress over injustice.

He starts by admitting how he almost lost his faith when he watched wicked people living healthy, carefree, prosperous lives while they kept mocking God and oppressing people. He says, "When I tried to understand all this, it troubled me deeply."[1]

It was only when he was in God's presence one day and had a vision of what the end looked like—what happened when God judged the wicked—that it all began to make sense.

But this was no theoretical, intellectual exercise. In a public confession to God, Asaph says:

---

1   Psalm 73:16.

When my heart was grieved
>and my spirit embittered,
I was senseless and ignorant;
>I was a brute beast before you.[2]

Even when injustice doesn't affect us personally, we can find it so offensive that it skews our view of God and undermines our relationship with him. So it's crucial that we deal with these feelings honestly and come to terms with the sovereign *timing* of God's judgment.

The apostle Peter, known for his impulsiveness while training as Jesus's disciple, offers a very different perspective years later in his letters. In regard to God's judgment, he urges us to take the long view:

> But do not forget this one thing, dear friends: With the Lord a day is like a thousand years, and a thousand years are like a day. The Lord is not slow in keeping his promise, as some understand slowness. Instead he is patient with you, not wanting anyone to perish, but everyone to come to repentance.[3]

Sometimes God waits (while we fume) because he wants to give more time for people to turn from their wrongdoing and be saved.

At other times, the situation apparently isn't bad enough yet.

Among the mysterious statements in the Bible, perhaps the most cryptic is one found in the book of Genesis where God is talking to Abram about the future. Referring to a time when Abram's descendants, the Israelites, would live in Egypt and eventually leave (the Exodus), God says: "In the fourth generation your descendants will

---

2   Psalm 73:21.

3   2 Peter 3:8-9.

come back here, for the sin of the Amorites has not yet reached its full measure."[4]

What does that tell us?

Judgment was coming for the Amorites, who were notorious for their idolatry, child sacrifices, religious prostitution, and divination. But not yet. Their sin had not yet reached its full measure. Whatever *that* means!

I'm sure Abram didn't nod his head and say, "Right, of course; I knew that." Neither do we need to pretend to know what a "full measure" of sin looks like in a particular culture over a number of centuries. Those issues are "above our pay grade," as the saying goes. They're in a category that only a sovereign God could assess.

And that "pay grade difference" (our understanding vs God's perspective) doesn't automatically disappear when we enter eternity. The Book of Revelation refers to a time when martyrs—Christians who have died for their faith—cry out to God for justice:

> "How long, Sovereign Lord, holy and true, until you judge the inhabitants of the earth and avenge our blood?" Then each of them was given a white robe, and they were told to wait a little longer, until the full number of their fellow servants, their brothers and sisters, were killed just as they had been.[5]

Again, there's reference to a full number and a waiting period before the judgment falls. Needless to say, there are no algorithms in math or physics for *that* kind of calculation.

Jesus once told a parable about a farmer planting good wheat seed. But then his enemy sneaks onto the field at night and sows

---

4 Genesis 15:16. Abram's name was later changed to *Abraham*.

5 Revelation 6:10-11.

weeds. When it becomes obvious that weeds are sprouting alongside the wheat, the owner is asked whether he wants the weeds pulled out.

"No," he answers, "because while you are pulling the weeds, you may uproot the wheat with them."

Jesus clearly does not want to see his people damaged through premature judgment, noting that at the end of the age "he will send out his angels, and they will weed out of his kingdom everything that causes sin and all who do evil."[6]

While the apostle Paul encourages churches to exercise judgment when dealing with obvious sin,[7] he also warns against presuming to know people's motives:

> Therefore judge nothing before the appointed time; wait until the Lord comes. He will bring to light what is hidden in darkness and will expose the motives of the heart. At that time each will receive their praise from God.[8]

When it comes to judgment, God may involve us, but remember: *he* makes the rules, and *he* has an "appointed time" that is exactly right.

Asaph the song leader eventually understood that, and could say with full conviction,

We praise you, God...

You say, "I choose the appointed time;

it is I who judge with equity."[9]

---

6   Matthew 13:24-30; 36-43.

7   Note 1 Corinthians chapters 5 and 6.

8   1 Corinthians 4:5.

9   Psalm 75:1-2.

Chapter 32

Running with Bulls and Angels
God's Sovereignty and Our Safety

This morning's news carried the story of the latest Running of the Bulls in Pamplona. On the first day only three people were gored sufficiently to require hospitalization, although fifty others (not counting the bulls) needed medical attention.

Whatever we may think of this annual weeklong event, it's still going strong after 800 years of such competitions in Spain. Concerns about cruel treatment of the bulls or foolhardy behavior by the runners isn't likely to change a tradition of that vintage.

So, what does a providential, caring God do when people deliberately engage in extremely risky (some would add, extremely stupid) behavior?

It wouldn't surprise me if some guardian angels were less charitable in their views on humanity than their Master. I could imagine a discussion taking place if, for example, their protection assignment included the Running of the Bulls...

Angel: "Just so I'm clear, you want me to protect this guy who is deliberately putting himself in harm's way in the most idiotic way—running down narrow streets in front of a bunch of charging bulls?"

Master: "That's correct."

Angel: "Despite the fact that he's doing it just to prove he's macho and to impress his immature friends?"

Master: "Exactly."

Angel: "But, with all due respect, why? Why wouldn't you just allow him to suffer the consequences of his foolish actions?"

Master: "There are reasons that not even you would understand. This man may not turn to me and be saved, but there are people among his descendants that are marked for my kingdom. So I want this man to live, and I don't want him disabled either."

Angel: "Understood. I will obey your will."

Of course, we don't really know whether our human foibles become a topic of discussion among the angels. If so, my name may have popped up the odd time.

Last summer a few of us "older types" were enjoying Okanagan Lake on a speedboat as our younger friends demonstrated how easy it was to waterski on a *Sky Ski* hydrofoil. In fact, it looked so easy I agreed to have a go—and also to try wakeboarding behind the boat.

There were many attempts, and just as many failures. After hitting the water multiple times, I felt like I had swallowed half the lake. But I had no idea some unseen damage was done (aside from a bruised ego).

The symptoms started slowly: dropping things, hitting the wrong keys on my laptop, and losing coordination in my left leg. Eventually a trip to Emergency resulted in a CT scan and a transfer to a larger hospital for neurosurgery, which involved drilling two holes in my skull to relieve the pressure of a brain bleed (subdural hematoma).[1]

During my recovery I felt gratitude for the blessing of our healthcare system and for the prayers and encouragement from friends and family,[2] but I also thought about how God had protected me from a worse outcome.

Probably the best-known promise of divine protection is found in the Psalms:

If you say, "The Lord is my refuge,"
　　　and you make the Most High your dwelling,
no harm will overtake you,
　　　no disaster will come near your tent.
For he will command his angels concerning you
　　　to guard you in all your ways;
they will lift you up in their hands,
　　　so that you will not strike your foot against a stone.[3]

So—exactly how are we to understand this promise? It sounds like an absolute guarantee of safety. Does it mean that if we're trusting God, we're somehow bubble-wrapped against injuries or calamities?

1　My brother said I needed that like a hole in the head—to which I replied I would then be holeyer than thou.

2　After the surgery, my daughters presented me with a cap with the inscription, *I've had brain surgery. What's your excuse?*—which I now wear whenever I play golf.

3　Psalm 91:9-12.

Not really. When the devil quoted this Scripture to Jesus in tempting him to jump off the highest point of the temple (presumably to impress people), Jesus answered with another Scripture: "Do not put the Lord your God to the test."[4]

Does that mean if we take undue risks, we're on our own? No. But since Jesus refers to deliberately dangerous behavior as "putting God to the test," we need to take his warning seriously.

Over the past few decades the *Darwin Awards* have found grisly humor in recognizing those who "eliminate themselves in an extraordinarily idiotic manner, thereby improving our species' chances of long-term survival."[5]

There is indeed humor in some of the crazy things people do to themselves, but, thankfully, God's approach is distinctly different:

The Lord is gracious and righteous;
our God is full of compassion.
The Lord protects the unwary;
when I was brought low, he saved me.[6]

If you check other translations of the phrase *protects the unwary*, you find examples like "preserves the simple," "guards the inexperienced," and "watches over the foolish."

I do want to learn from my mistakes and avoid presuming on God's protection. But I'm very thankful that he "protects the unwary." (I wouldn't be around to write this if he didn't.)

---

4   Deuteronomy 6:16.

5   https://en.wikipedia.org/wiki/Darwin_Awards.

6   Psalm 116:5-6.

Chapter 33

The Mysteries of Misery
Sovereignty, Pain, and Suffering (Part 1)

Confession: I am not one of those heroic souls who handle aches and pains stoically. At the first sign of a headache, I'm likely to pop a pill in order to stop the pain before it gets any worse.

Some say, *No pain, no gain.* I identify more with the proposition, *No pain, no pain.*

I suppose we make jokes about pain because suffering is universal, and we all find ways of coping with it. I'm reminded of a line from the movie *Princess Bride* when the hero Westley tells Princess Buttercup, "Life is pain, Highness. Anyone who says differently is selling something."[1]

Young Westley may have overstated it, but it's undeniable that sooner or later we all deal with life's woes, whether physical, mental, emotional, spiritual, or relational.

---

1   Rob Reiner, dir., *Princess Bride* (1987; Beverly Hills, CA: Twentieth Century Fox, 2015), DVD.

A brief chapter or two on this subject is obviously inadequate, but I do want to share a few key truths that have helped on my own journey through grief and trouble.[2] Some deal with the *Why?* questions; others focus on how a sovereign God interacts with human suffering:

- *Why is there suffering when God is both loving and all-powerful?*

This is a question both Christians and non-Christians have wrestled with for thousands of years. C.S. Lewis, a former atheist himself, identifies the source of suffering as *evil*, and says evil is made possible by the free will God gave people:

> Why, then, did God give them free will? Because free will, though it makes evil possible, is also the only thing that makes possible any love or goodness or joy worth having.[3]

In other words, God's decision to create human beings instead of robots created the potential for much good, but also the opportunity for people to make bad choices, resulting in suffering.

- *Since God is both sovereign and good, why doesn't he stop the pain when we ask him to?*

Sometimes God does answer our cries of distress promptly, but not always. And we don't necessarily know why. There may not even be an earthly reason for it. In the case of Job, who suffered pain on every imaginable level over an extended period of time, the main issue apparently was God wanting to prove a point to Satan!

---

2   Several books listed in the bibliography offer a more comprehensive treatment of pain and suffering.

3   C.S. Lewis, *The Best of C.S. Lewis: The Case for Christianity* (Washington, DC: Canon Press, 1969), 436.

It may seem callous to say it, but the truth is: we are not *owed* a pain-free life. Even someone as righteous as Job, who clearly felt he didn't deserve his troubles and misery, had no right to demand relief from God.

One solace (limited though it may be) is that pain and suffering are temporary, not permanent conditions. We may experience reprieve from suffering in this life, but only heaven spells the end of heartache, torment, pain, and affliction. Forever.

Mother Teresa said it well:

> In light of heaven, the worst suffering on earth, a life full of the most atrocious tortures on earth, will be seen to be no more serious than one night in an inconvenient hotel.[4]

- *Does God actually care about our suffering?*

We may be inclined to think that since God knows the big picture, he is unmoved by our suffering. Nothing could be further from the truth.

When Jesus was contacted by his friends Mary and Martha to heal their brother Lazarus, he delayed his arrival several days so that Lazarus would die. Why? Because he planned to raise him from the dead.

Nevertheless, the sorrow Jesus witnessed at the gravesite was enough to make him weep too. Scripture says he was "deeply moved," [5] a Greek term referring to loud expressions of grief. He entered into their suffering despite knowing he was going to change it all.

Now, we might assume God's response is different when someone *deserves* to suffer. Maybe we think he rubs his hands in glee when the

---

4   https://www.goodreads.com/
      quotes/633279-in-light-of-heaven-the-worst-suffering-on-earth-a.

5   John 11:33-38.

bad guy gets his due. (Some of us can relate to that kind of satisfaction while watching certain movies.)

But here's how he actually feels about it:

> "Do I take any pleasure in the death of the wicked?" declares the Sovereign Lord. "Rather, am I not pleased when they turn from their ways and live?"[6]

Recalling Israel's checkered history, the prophet Isaiah speaks of God's tender response in the midst of their oft-deserved troubles: "In all their distress he too was distressed."[7] (Somehow, that statement impacts me even more than verses about God's overwhelming power.)

We'll close this chapter with the ultimate example of God entering into human suffering—as revealed in Isaiah's prophecies about the coming Christ:

Surely he took up our pain
and bore our suffering,
yet we considered him punished by God,
stricken by him, and afflicted.
But he was pierced for our transgressions,
he was crushed for our iniquities;
the punishment that brought us peace was on him,
and by his wounds we are healed.[8]

---

6   Ezekiel 18:23.

7   Isaiah 63:9.

8   Isaiah 53:4-5.

Chapter 34

Is There Meaning in Tragedy?
Sovereignty, Pain, and Suffering (Part 2)

Even if we agreed that pain and suffering were due to humanity's evil choices, we'd suspect there was more to it.

- *Our bad decisions—people exercising their free will the wrong way—might explain 80% or even 90% of evil, but what about natural disasters or unavoidable disease?*

According to New York pastor/author Timothy Keller, this question wasn't always the big issue it is today.

To put it into historical perspective, he refers to philosopher Charles Taylor's description that we now live inside an "immanent frame," viewing the world as a completely natural order without any supernatural,[1] and he points to the rise of Deism in the 18th century:

> The idea of Deism is that God created the world for our benefit and now it operates on its own, without his constant

---

1   Timothy Keller, Walking with God Through Pain and Suffering (New York, NY: Penguin Books, 2013), 53.

or direct involvement... In short, the older Christian idea that we exist for God's glory receded and was replaced by the belief that God exists to nurture and sustain us.[2]

We've probably heard snide remarks about the *Me* generation, but according to some commentators, that really describes every generation.[3] Why? Because our natural inclination is to think *it's all about me!* Except that it actually isn't.

According to the Bible, "all things have been created through him and for him."[4] And who is the "him" that Scripture is talking about? *Jesus Christ.* All things—including all of us—were created not only through him but *for* him.

(Truth be told, I often forget that "little" fact.)

Timothy Keller goes on to say, "If you believe that the world was made for our benefit by God, then horrendous suffering and evil will shake your understanding of life."[5] Sooner or later, we all experience tragedy. What then? If God doesn't explain himself to us, will we become bitter and lose our faith?

There certainly are examples in the Bible of God telling prophets the reasons for upcoming wars and famine, but the warnings were seldom heeded. Jesus told his disciples before he was crucified what was coming, but they didn't understand it until after his resurrection.[6]

More often than not, tragedies occur without divine explanation. There is no record of God telling Job why he let him suffer, let alone why he allowed a natural disaster to kill his children. In fact, when

2   Keller, 54.
3   https://www.theatlantic.com/national/archive/2013/05/
     me-generation-time/315151/.
4   Colossians 1:16.
5   Keller, *Walking with God*, 56.
6   Luke 18:31-34; 24:13-49.

God finally did speak, it seemed like the ultimate non sequitur—four long chapters describing the wonders of his creation!

But in the end, as Job gains a new awareness of God's greatness and sovereignty, he stops expecting God to explain, and humbly says, "Surely I spoke of things I did not understand, / things too wonderful for me to know."[7]

Mike Mason, in his magnificent study on the book of Job, sees faith as something we can offer God—just as the apostle Paul encourages us to "offer every part of yourself to him as an instrument of righteousness."[8]

> But probably the last of all the parts to be wholly offered is our intellect, our compulsive need to comprehend everything, to create a sense of reasonable order where none is apparent. Yet why should we expect life to be reasonable? It is the Lord who is sovereign, not human reason. While faith is not contrary to reason, it does greatly surpass it.[9]

- *When suffering seems arbitrary and unrelenting, how can we know there's meaning or purpose in it?*

If ever there was a situation where unrelenting suffering held sway, it was in Nazi concentration camps during World War II. Among the inmates in Germany were two Dutch women, Corrie ten Boom and her sister Betsie, who had been sentenced for hiding Jews from the Gestapo. As Betsie lay dying, she whispered to her sister that they must tell others what they had learned about the Lord:

---

7   Job 42:3.

8   Romans 6:13.

9   Mike Mason, The Gospel According to Job (Wheaton, Illinois: Crossway, 1994), 424.

We must tell them that there is no pit so deep that He is not deeper still. They will listen to us, Corrie, because we have been here.[10]

Betsie died, but soon after, Corrie ten Boom was released (apparently due to a clerical error) while all the other women her age were sent to the gas chambers. After the war, she was instrumental in bringing healing to victims of the war, sharing the message of peace and reconciliation through Christ in over 60 countries.

Philip Yancey, who has written extensively on suffering, points to the vital role of hope and faith:

> We have no more definitive answer than Job got. We have only stubborn hope—so different from naïve optimism—that the story of Jesus, which includes both death and resurrection, gives a bright clue to what God will do for the entire planet...Faith, I've concluded, means believing in advance what will only make sense in reverse."[11]

Why does God permit a tragedy? We sometimes understand it at the time, but often we don't. That's when faith is sorely tested, but it's also when we have something unique to offer: our trust in a God who is all-wise, all-merciful, and almighty.

---

10   Corrie ten Boom, *The Hiding Place* (New York, NY: Bantam Books, 1974), 217.

11   Philip Yancey, *The Question That Never Goes Away* (Grand Rapids, Michigan: Zondervan, 2013), 47-48.

Chapter 35

On Hold with Heaven
God's Sovereign Timing

It was a small detail, but it caught my eye.

I was reading about the time King David had the brilliant idea of building a temple. But through the prophet Nathan, God told David that he wasn't the right man to build the temple; instead, his son Solomon would be. And then God says, "But my love will never be taken away from him, as I took it away from Saul, whom I removed from before you."[1]

That last phrase got me thinking. The record does show that years earlier, God had commissioned Samuel to anoint David as the next king, and then proceeded to remove Saul. But do you know how long the removal process took? About 15 years. We sometimes get impatient when God's answer takes more than 15 minutes!

It gets worse.

Abraham and his wife Sarah were childless for a long time—decades, in fact—which was a great sorrow to them. But then God

---

1   2 Samuel 7:15.

promised them a son who would be the rightful heir and whose lineage would include countless descendants in a land of promise.

And how long was it until their son Isaac was born? About 25 years. Sarah was well past childbearing age by then, and didn't really believe it could happen, but it did.

Fast-forward to the time when God called Moses at the burning bush and gave him this encouraging message:

> I have indeed seen the misery of my people in Egypt. I have heard them crying out because of their slave drivers, and I am concerned about their suffering. So I have come down to rescue them from the hand of the Egyptians..."[2]

A bit of context may help us understand the situation. The oppression of the Israelites would have begun before Moses's time (given the circumstances of his birth when Israelite baby boys were to be killed). If it started just twenty years before Moses's birth, that would add up to a *century* of harsh slavery, as Moses was 80 years old at the Exodus.

Now consider the prayers of devout Israelites in response to this oppression—prayers that seemed to have gone unheard and unanswered for a hundred years! And yet God says to Moses, "I have heard them crying out because of their slave drivers, and I am concerned about their suffering."

Is there a disconnect here? If you were an Israelite who lived and died within that century, would you think God had heard your prayers and was concerned about your suffering?

This chapter focuses on timing, but it could also be about faith, couldn't it? What does God expect of us when we see no response to our cry for help? Can we even imagine a scenario where he's hearing

---

2   Exodus 3:7-8.

and answering, but doing so on a different time scale because of purposes we can't comprehend?

> Imagine for a moment that God decided to explain things to an Israelite slave during that time. Putting it in human terms, it might go something like this:
>
> *Look, I'm concerned about your situation, even if you don't see evidence of that. I have a Promised Land for you in Canaan. However, I know the Israelites will never leave Egypt until there's enough pressure over enough time that they're motivated to go. (Even then there will be an attempt to return to Egypt.[3]) Your children will be part of the great Exodus, but your own life on earth will come to an end before then. This is a time of suffering but it's necessary, and it won't be wasted if you keep trusting me.*

We have no record of any such conversation, of course, and it's only in retrospect that we could suggest reasons for some things God does or doesn't do.

The issue is: Will we acknowledge God's sovereignty when it comes to timing? Will we trust that he is always faithful, always loving, all-wise, and all-powerful, even when many years go by without seeing answers?

Luke's Gospel starts with the story of John the Baptist, which begins with a childless couple, Zechariah and Elizabeth, waiting for answers to prayer—and getting very old in the meantime.

Eventually they give up—at least, that's what the story suggests.

Zechariah, a priest chosen to burn incense in front of the Most Holy Place, witnesses the appearance of the angel Gabriel, who says, among other things, "Your prayer has been heard. Your wife

---

3   Numbers 14:3-4.

Elizabeth will bear you a son, and you are to call him John"—but he doesn't believe it.[4]

For God and his messenger Gabriel, the issue of time doesn't seem to matter. This was the answer to the couple's prayers—even if it was 30 or 40 years after they had started praying. Even if it was years since they'd *stopped* praying that prayer!

We can never assume that God is not answering our prayers just because weeks, months, years, and even decades go by without seeing the answer. God's timetable is not like ours. And for him it's never too late.

As someone with experience in waiting for God's promise, King David offers us this counsel when we feel like we're "on hold" with Heaven:

Wait for the Lord;

be strong and take heart

and wait for the Lord.[5]

---

4   Luke 1:5-25.

5   Psalm 27:14.

Chapter 36

A Poor Substitute
Sovereignty and Temptation

The most unflattering descriptions of the devil I've come across were spoken by the most gracious person who ever lived—Jesus Christ.

Of course, Jesus spoke from first-hand knowledge because he is the eternal Son of God through whom all things were created[1]—including Lucifer, who was a mighty celestial being before he fell from grace and became known as Satan or the devil.

Here's what Jesus once said to his opponents who were looking for a way to destroy him:

> You belong to your father, the devil, and you want to carry out your father's desires. He was a murderer from the beginning, not holding to the truth, for there is no truth in him. When he lies, he speaks his native language, for he is a liar and the father of lies."[2]

---

1   Colossians 1:15-16.

2   John 8:44.

Not much ambiguity or diplomacy there! In another reference to the devil, Jesus says, "The thief comes only to steal and kill and destroy."[3]

The nature of our enemy is unmistakably evil, cruel, and destructive. His approach, on the other hand, can seem quite benign, especially when he drops reasonable-sounding suggestions and offers interesting temptations. He's brilliant in the art of making sin look inviting.

But there's always a hidden agenda. Temptations are never designed to bring us something beneficial, even if sin may offer a transitory thrill. They are intended to rob us—and those connected to us—of what is best.

The fact is: Satan is incapable of offering anything better than what God has to offer. Scripture says, "Every good and perfect gift is from above, coming down from the Father…"[4] The best that Satan can offer is a poor substitute for the real thing.

Because Satan cannot actually create anything, his approach is to suggest alternatives to God's ways. In that sense he's inventive, but he's also the ultimate con artist. He doesn't supply small-print disclaimers explaining the side effects of those deviations.

His modus operandi in the Garden of Eden is the same today: trying to get people to believe he's got something outside of God's will that's worth having. (In all honesty, I find it hard to believe how I've fallen for that line myself.)

He might even suggest (without putting it into these exact words) that because God forgives sin, we can have the best of both worlds—Jesus and sin—as if "best" could ever be applied to the world of sin!

But it's not only that we allow ourselves to be robbed when we fall for temptation, we also impair our relationship with the One

---

3   John 10:10.

4   James 1:17.

who loves us and gave his life for us. Just as the first human couple hid themselves from God after they sinned, we also tend to keep our distance from God when we feel guilt and shame—which is exactly what the enemy wants, if for no other reason than that our faith level plummets at such times.

So, is sin ever worth it? What a question! Of course not. But there's part of me that sometimes begs to differ.[5] Sometimes truth is swept aside by our compulsions, addictions, fears, or bad habits, and we fall into the enemy's snare. What then? Does God's sovereignty still apply?

Absolutely.

Firstly, we can be assured that temptation is *not* irresistible. According to Scripture, God sets the boundaries for it:

> No temptation has overtaken you except what is common to mankind. And God is faithful; he will not let you be tempted beyond what you can bear. But when you are tempted, he will also provide a way out so that you can endure it.[6]

Secondly, if we do sin (and there is no one who does not sin[7]), God provides the answer:

> If we confess our sins, he is faithful and just and will forgive us our sins and purify us from all unrighteousness.[8]

---

5   That was also the apostle Paul's experience, as described in Romans chapter 7.

6   1 Corinthians 10:13.

7   1 Kings 8:46; Romans 3:23.

8   1 John 1:9.

Thirdly, God provides grace for us to draw on so that we can live in freedom. As Jesus said, "If the Son sets you free, you will be free indeed."[9]

Jesus set many people free when he walked this earth, and he still does today. How? Through means of grace like Scripture, prayer, confession, forgiveness (receiving forgiveness and forgiving others), healing, deliverance from evil spirits, discipleship (being accountable and learning in the context of a small group), and being filled with the Holy Spirit.

The truth is: while sin masquerades as something clever, powerful, and pervasive, it is actually foolish, weak, and short-lived compared to God's eternal kingdom. The best Satan can offer is a poor substitute for the good things God has created.

We'll give the last word to the apostle Peter, a man who didn't always resist temptation, but who in later years wrote this grand statement on what his Master, Jesus, offers us:

> His divine power has given us everything we need for a godly life through our knowledge of him who called us by his own glory and goodness.[10]

---

9   John 8:36.

10   2 Peter 1:3.

Chapter 37

Heavenly Parties
Sovereignty and God's Emotions (Part 1)

One of the best-loved characters on the original Star Trek TV series was first officer of the Starship Enterprise, Mr. Spock, whose emotionless logic in the midst of crises stood in stark contrast to the sometimes-irascible Captain Kirk.

I have to admit, I tended to admire that character trait, and subconsciously imagined it reflected what God must be like: serenely unaffected by the ups and downs and clamor of this messy, emotional world. But that's not how the Bible describes God. And it's quite different from what Jesus was like.

Jesus once told a series of parables (stories) that share a common theme: the *Lost Sheep* (where one sheep wanders off and the shepherd leaves the remaining flock of ninety-nine sheep to go rescue it); the *Lost Coin* (where a woman celebrates finding a coin that was lost); and the *Lost Son* (a prodigal who gets into a mess and finally returns home, hoping to find help—but not expecting acceptance).

In each case there is an emphasis on the joy that follows when something is lost but finally is found. In fact, Jesus goes so far as to say, "I tell you that in the same way there will be more rejoicing in heaven over one sinner who repents than over ninety-nine righteous persons who do not need to repent."[1]

Now, it's understandable if human beings respond that way to the lost being found, given the intense focus of the search—but how does this square with what we know of God?

We mortals easily lose perspective when we're emotionally charged, but God is perfect and never loses perspective. Then how do we explain "more rejoicing in heaven over one sinner who repents"? Should we go out and sin and then repent, just so there will be more rejoicing in heaven?

The apostle Paul once raised a similar question:

> What then? Shall we sin because we are not under the law but under grace? By no means! Don't you know that when you offer yourselves to someone as obedient slaves, you are slaves of the one you obey—whether you are slaves to sin, which leads to death, or to obedience, which leads to righteousness?[2]

So, if Jesus's statement about joy in heaven isn't mainly about sinning and repenting, what's the key issue?

It's relationship.

Jesus is showing us how much value God places on a human life. The prodigal's older brother saw him as a useless wastrel, but to the father he was a precious member of the family; thus the father's insistence that they celebrate his homecoming.

Of course, Jesus wasn't just telling stories for entertainment. He was talking about *us*. When we consider the enormity of the sacrifice God made in sending Jesus to die for us—so that we might be

---

1   Luke 15:7.

2   Romans 6:15-16.

restored to the Father—how could we not celebrate the return of any prodigal?

Isn't it great that we have a God who loves to celebrate? Just think of the fact that Jesus's first miracle was turning about 120 gallons of water into wine at a wedding feast![3]

What kinds of occasions spark joy in heaven? What are their excuses for a party?

- when a sinner is saved and brought into relationship with God and his eternal family (huge celebrations for that!)
- when a Christian passes from this life and enters God's presence
- times when we endure trials and temptations with grace and faith
- when God's people work through their conflicts, forgiving and accepting each other
- when injustice and other evils are overcome—whether on a personal or societal level
- a man and woman finding each other and getting married in covenant love
- a new life (baby) coming to birth
- medical and scientific discoveries being birthed, whether in a lab, a particle accelerator, or the mind of a brilliant mathematician

That last point may not seem like something heaven would get excited about, but Scripture speaks of celebrations being triggered by God's creation of the earth: "…the morning stars sang together and all the angels shouted for joy."[4] There is no reason to think

---

3   John 2:1-11.

4   Job 38:7.

that angels have lost their wonder for those works of God—and nor should we.

But while heaven's inhabitants find a variety of reasons to celebrate, God's main focus is still on relationships. He has not revealed himself as a bureaucratic manager who carefully doles out his love and grace in equal measure, but rather as an exuberant Father who welcomes his family to himself with great joy and celebration, even when, like the prodigal son, we have wandered far from him and return penniless and dissolute.

The reality is: sometimes we're part of the ninety-nine, and sometimes we're the one sheep that he goes out to rescue because we've wandered away.

I'm glad that when he rescues you and me, he's not angry because of our foolishness, and he's not emotionless like Spock. But he's joyful, welcoming, and just waiting to start the celebration.

Chapter 38

From Bliss to Blues
Sovereignty and God's Emotions (Part 2)

In a study published in 2017, researchers at the University of California identified 27 distinct categories of emotions.[1]

Who knew? Some of us (mostly on the male side of the ledger, I suspect) think we're doing well to recognize three or four.

Truth be told, I've tended to regard emotions with a certain wariness most of my life. Emotions can be so irrational, so unpredictable, so unconstrained, so raw. And yet life would be quite flat and boring without them.

By God's grace I've been able to grow in this regard, at least in terms of being more in touch with what's going on inside. My soul isn't quite the black hole it once was, where, like its cosmic counterpart, no information or light seemed to escape.

---

1   https://www.forbes.com/sites/brucelee/2017/09/09/here-are-the-27-different-human-emotions-according-to-a-study/#4a6bbea61335.

That type of growth is important for everyone, male or female, not only for the sake of our health and well-being, but also for the purpose of expressing more fully how God made us.

He made us in his image—which includes the capacity for healthy emotional expression. God is very clear about how *he* feels about certain people and things:

- "I am the Lord who exercises kindness, / justice and righteousness on earth, / for in these I delight," declares the Lord.[2]
- When the Lord heard them, he was furious / his fire broke out against Jacob / and his wrath rose against Israel / for they did not believe in God / or trust in his deliverance.[3]
- "For I, the Lord, love justice / I hate robbery and wrongdoing."[4]
- As a bridegroom rejoices over his bride / so will your God rejoice over you.[5]

When it comes to emotions, we often struggle to understand God. We tend either to "anthropomorphize" him—imagining him to be just like us in our responses—or to picture him as completely removed from our experience of joy, sorrow, anger, and so on.

And sometimes we forget that since he inhabits both time and eternity, he can connect with us on our timeline in a way that is interactive, empathetic, and real.

The Bible portrays God as a Person with a full range of emotions (no doubt beyond the 27 identified in the California study), but

2   Jeremiah 9:24.

3   Psalm 78:21-22.

4   Isaiah 61:8.

5   Isaiah 62:5.

there are clear differences. For one thing, his emotions are never in conflict with his integrity, holiness, sovereignty, love, mercy, or any other aspect of his character.

And his emotions are never out of control. He doesn't lose his temper, nor is he swayed by sentimentality or our attempts to manipulate him. In a sobering statement of judgment through the prophet Jeremiah, God declares at one point, "I will allow no pity or mercy or compassion to keep me from destroying them."[6]

Because he knows everything, God can even predict how he is *going* to react emotionally, as we see in this prophecy about a time in Israel's future: "Then my anger will cease and my wrath against them will subside."[7]

There's full knowledge and full control when it comes to God's emotions. But that doesn't mean his feelings are somehow less than what we experience. We may have entire music genres like the blues to express our pain and sorrow, but God has his own version of that right in the Bible.

If you've ever read the Old Testament prophets like Isaiah, Jeremiah, Ezekiel, and Hosea, you can't help but be impacted by the strength of God's concern for his people who were turning to evil on a massive scale and refusing to heed any warnings. That left only one option—extreme judgment—and we see God's emotional response range from sadness to joy, from anger to love, from fury to longing and tenderness.

The fact that we have a book of the Bible called *Lamentations* tells us that suffering and judgment are no trivial matters to God. The writer of the book was Jeremiah, but the real Author was God, who inspired laments like this:

My eyes fail from weeping,

---

6   Jeremiah 13:14.

7   Ezekiel 5:13.

I am in torment within;
my heart is poured out on the ground
because my people are destroyed.[8]

If we view these judgments simply as punishment, we will have missed the point. God's justice certainly is a factor, but it's much more than that—especially when it involves his people Israel.

God knew that if he allowed them to continue down the path of evil—idol worship, violence, child sacrifice, injustice, and oppression—they would completely destroy themselves. He didn't inflict judgment on them because he hated them, but precisely because he loved them too much to let them stagger to their doom.

Emotion, even in God's case, often comes down to relationship—caring enough about people that he's willing to speak the truth even when it hurts, and to intervene if that's ultimately what it takes.

Emotion expresses what we value most. If tears at a wedding service are any indicator, a loving, committed, covenant relationship tops the list for many people.

Is that a reflection of our Creator? Absolutely.

Our sovereign God, the Supreme Being, determines what's supremely important—and *whom* he considers valuable.

Have you ever asked him how he feels about you?[9]

---

8   Lamentations 2:11.

9   You may want to have a tissue handy!

Chapter 39

The Right to Look
Sovereignty and Sex

There we were with a tour group on the original Mount Zion, City of David in Jerusalem, where the king's palace once stood.

On the hillside immediately below us, the guide explained, was where David's mighty men—his generals—lived, one of whom was Uriah the Hittite. And suddenly it became clear how, one fateful evening long ago, King David spied Uriah's wife bathing.

If you've read the story, you know David made a bad choice. He kept on looking, and then had her brought to him. And then tried to cover up what he had done.[1]

Here in the 21st century, in a world rife with scandals, leaks, hacked emails, and hidden cameras, a key concern for those trying to hide something is whether their embarrassing

---

1   2 Samuel chapter 11.

behavior will be splashed all over news networks and social media platforms.

King David had no such worries. But little did he know that the story of his lust, adultery, and murderous cover-up would be written up in Scripture and become known to billions of people in the centuries that followed.

Why, we might ask, would the Almighty expose such a sordid chapter in the life of someone he called "a man after the heart of God"? It could only be because of the lessons to be learned.

One of those lessons is that adultery is wrong because it is theft.

When Nathan the prophet confronts David about his adultery, he tells a story about a rich man taking a lamb from a poor man—which causes the king to react with righteous indignation—that is, until Nathan points to David and tells him *he's* the rich man in that story!

So it's clear that God regards adultery as stealing from someone else's spouse. But it goes further. Nathan says, "Why did you despise the word of the Lord…?" and David ultimately admits, "I have sinned against the Lord."[2]

Why exactly is it a sin against the Lord?

The obvious answer is that it violates God's law. But the issue goes beyond that. It has to do with the unseen but fundamental reality that God is the *Owner* of everyone and everything.[3] If I commit adultery, I'm not only taking what belongs to someone else, I'm also stealing from the ultimate Owner, namely God.

But it doesn't end there.

---

2   2 Samuel 12:9-13.

3   Psalm 24:1.

What if I don't commit adultery but allow myself the option of "looking"? Do I have the right to do that?

Or what if I'm not stealing a look (as in spying on someone), but just enjoying the view that someone is offering—whether online, in movies, or otherwise? Isn't that just appreciating God's creation and not hurting anyone?

Well, here are the words of Jesus:

> You have heard that it was said, "You shall not commit adultery." But I tell you that anyone who looks at a woman lustfully has already committed adultery with her in his heart.[4]

If God ultimately owns us, that means we don't have the right to display our bodies, nor the right to view other people's bodies (outside of marriage) in ways the Owner doesn't approve—any more than we have the right to receive stolen goods.

It would be as if a hired clerk in a jewelry store were to give a customer some diamond rings and bracelets under the counter and say, "Go ahead; you can have these." An honest customer would reply, "But you have no right to give them, and I have no right to receive them. It would be theft."

Now, even if all of that makes sense, and we agree that sex belongs exclusively within marriage, it doesn't necessarily make it easy to live by the standards set by Jesus. *Knowing* truth doesn't automatically give us the power to live by it. (I, for one, can attest to that!) So I'm grateful for the Holy Spirit and resources like books, seminars, and accountability groups that help us learn how to live out the truth we believe.

---

4   Matthew 5:27-28.

The Bible isn't squeamish about any subject, including sex. David's wrongdoing in that regard is told directly and honestly. And while the painful consequences are recounted, so is the fact that sexual sins are not beyond the scope of God's forgiveness and restoration.

We're all capable of falling into sin, whether in major wrongdoing or what we think of as minor misdeeds. That's when we need to remember what Scripture says about Jesus:

> For we do not have a high priest who is unable to empathize with our weaknesses, but we have one who has been tempted in every way, just as we are—yet he did not sin. Let us then approach God's throne of grace with confidence, so that we may receive mercy and find grace to help us in our time of need.[5]

Living in the reality of God's sovereignty may start with acknowledging Jesus's Lordship over our bodies and minds, but it includes approaching him with confidence, knowing that he empathizes with our weaknesses, and offers us the help we need. What a gracious invitation!

---

5   Hebrews 4:15-16.

Chapter 40

Image of God
Sovereignty and Racism

Not since airliners crashed into New York's Twin Towers on 9/11 had an image so impacted America: a white police officer kneeling on the neck of a handcuffed African American man—a brutal act lasting for over nine minutes until George Floyd was dead.

The outrage that followed was swift and violent, exposing a racial divide that most Americans had hoped was long resolved.

Growing up in the 1950s and 60s in British Columbia, Canada, I thought racism was something *other* countries dealt with, especially after reading books like *Why We Can't Wait* by Martin Luther King, Jr. and *Black Like Me* by John Howard Griffin.[1]

That impression was reinforced years later when I attended a Promise Keepers conference for 80,000 men at the Seattle Kingdome. During one session, the speaker shared a powerful message and then invited men who were prepared to renounce their racist attitudes to

---

1   In *Black Like Me*, a white journalist recounts how he darkened his skin and then traveled around the American South as a black person.

come forward. I was shocked to see men by the thousands streaming to the front for confession and prayer.

Fast-forward to a conversation among family and friends just a few years ago on Canada Day. When someone referred to the beginning of our country's history in the 1500s, someone else challenged it, pointing out that those dates only referred to the arrival of Europeans, as the original inhabitants of this land had been here for thousands of years. I'm embarrassed to admit that this was an aha moment for me.

Of course, I remembered those facts from school, but the mindset of what constituted our history's starting point revealed an unconscious bias. The Indigenous peoples somehow did not count.[2]

Speaking of mindset, have you ever wondered why north is always *up* on maps and globes? From a strictly scientific standpoint, it would be just as correct to have south on top, as any astronaut circling the earth could confirm.

North is up mainly because European superpowers dominated much of the known world in the 16th century, and mapmakers obligingly put Europe—and the rest of the northern hemisphere—on top.[3]

Have we inherited that mindset without realizing it? Do we think God looks at the earth with the same orientation we have arbitrarily assigned to it?

The truth is: all of us are affected by the biases we've grown up with and the perspectives we've been taught. Which is why it's vitally important to approach a subject like racism from God's frame of reference.

---

2   According to government estimates, Indigenous peoples numbering around 500,000 lived in "Canada" in the late 15th century.

3   https://www.geospatialworld.net/blogs/why-maps-point-north-on-top/.

If God is sovereign, then it's *his* viewpoint that's relevant, not our biases—nor our clumsy attempts to shed them. And what is God's viewpoint? An all-important clue is found in the creation account:

So God created mankind in his own image,

in the image of God he created them;

male and female he created them.[4]

Nature is filled with displays of beauty and power. But only humans were created in God's own image. Men and women represent the pinnacle of his creation.

It's important to note that the image of God is generally understood to refer to non-physical attributes such as our intellect, imagination, creativity, spirituality, and conscience (moral code).

Still, do we have any idea of what Adam and Eve might have looked like? Perhaps. Most scientists believe the first (modern) humans lived in Africa, which suggests they probably didn't resemble pictures we may have seen in Sunday School:

> Scientific data indicates that the first humans looked very much like African people groups today. Heavy (dark) skin pigmentation offered protection against the harmful effects of UV radiation in hot, southern latitudes and prevented the loss of folic acid.[5]

That said, it shouldn't really matter which race or ethnic group the first humans looked like, since God eventually chose to create a wide array of people types. The point? God demonstrates his glory in the diversity of things, plants, animals, and people he creates. Since that is a key value for our Creator, we creatures need to follow suit.

---

4   Genesis 1:27.

5   Fazale Rana with Hugh Ross, *Who Was Adam? A Creation Model Approach to the Origin of Humanity,* 2nd expanded edition (Covina, California: Reasons to Believe, 2015), 364.

To criticize his handiwork, especially people made in his own image, is like disparaging Leonardo da Vinci's *Mona Lisa* or Michelangelo's *David*—only worse.

Racism is telling people they are inferior—worth *less* than others. It damages them at a deep level of their soul. But even more outrageous is how it insults Almighty God— basically telling him we don't appreciate his image in certain people groups.

Viewed in that light, racism is worse than even a radical activist could imagine. Which means we need God's help. So we pray these words of David from the Psalms:

But who can discern their own errors?

Forgive my hidden faults.[6]

Show me your ways, Lord,

teach me your paths.[7]

Only the God who deliberately made people with *differences* can show us how to relate to and honor one another—and thus honor his sovereignty as Creator.

---

6   Psalm 19:12.

7   Psalm 25:4.

Chapter 41

Just Between You and God
Sovereignty, Relationships, and Time

Of the many qualities that impress me about my wife, I would single out her extraordinary capacity for communication.

I see that gift in her teaching roles, in parenting and grandparenting, in extending hospitality to guests, and in extracting key concepts from all the books she reads.

But one example stands out—at least, for me—whenever we host a friend whom she got to know years ago as a college roommate. No matter how many hours the two of them may have already spent in conversation, early next morning I'll hear their muffled voices downstairs, engrossed in deep discussion. And every time, I think to myself, *What could they possibly find to talk about for all those hours?*[1]

The point is that we cannot imagine a friendship existing apart from communication. And since communication (in our experience)

---

1   For the record, I know it's not idle gossip, but rather in-depth discussion about people, God, and various spiritual and societal issues.

always happens within a time frame, we can't really imagine relationship outside of time.

So, how does it work when we're dealing with a Supreme Being who transcends time? If communication requires time—as in *Person A* commenting or asking a question, and then *Person B* responding—how can we converse with a God who doesn't live on our timeline?

There's another problem: How can we engage in meaningful conversation with someone who knows everything we're going to say? Are we kidding ourselves to think that a human being can talk with the Supreme Being? And if we do have such a conversation (i.e. when we pray) and we hear a response, is he just humoring us as a parent would indulge a two-year-old?

In other words, is our communication with God real? Does God even *want* that level of engagement with the likes of you and me, or is he too busy running the universe?

Before trying to answer that, we would do well to acknowledge an obvious limitation—namely, our inability to grasp the infinite wisdom and power of Almighty God. We may have some concept of infinity from the study of mathematics or theology, but we can't grasp its full meaning. Even the brainiest among us are incapable of that.

Regarding time, a key point is that the Creator of space and time inhabits both time and eternity and therefore can relate to us in either sphere.

Here on planet Earth, many physicists have adopted "string theory" as a way of explaining how the universe works, with models that include hidden dimensions of space—beyond the three dimensions we're familiar with—as well as hidden dimensions of time. If such a model is correct, we can safely assume that God inhabits *all* the dimensions of space and time he created.[2]

Thankfully, we don't need to understand quantum gravity to relate to God. In fact, he makes himself known to children and the uneducated as much as he does to those of towering intellect (maybe more so). Regardless, it's worth grappling with the issue of how we relate to an infinite God, because that's the most important relationship anyone could ever have.

Speaking of grappling, we often use the word metaphorically, as opposed to the literal grappling that wrestlers do. But there's a strange story in Genesis chapter 32 about Jacob wrestling with the angel of God, and the angel eventually giving him the name Israel, which carried the meaning, "he struggles with God."

The Bible is full of stories about people who struggled with God, if not physically then mentally, emotionally, and spiritually: Job, Abraham, Jacob, Moses, Elijah, David, Jeremiah, Peter, Paul, even Nicodemus.

To put it another way, they *engaged* with God.

While others gave in to fear, disappointment, and unbelief, these people chose to engage God, even during painful and perplexing times. As a result, they established a close relationship and fulfilled their destiny.

For some, the idea that a sovereign God would actually engage us in a personal way seems a little too fantastic to be taken seriously. Yet the record of both the Jewish and Christian Scriptures is all about such engagement. In fact, one of the best-known names in Old Testament prophecy for the coming Christ was *Immanuel,* meaning *God with us.*

---

2   For an exploration of how string theory may interact with theology (and help explain certain paradoxes) see Hugh Ross: *Beyond the Cosmos: The Transdimensionality of God,* Third Edition (Covina, CA: rtbpress, 2017).

For reasons we can't comprehend (except love, which is itself beyond explanation), he wants to engage us, and he wants us to engage him. He might even be looking for a relationship that's more like the one I've observed between my wife and her long-time friend—where there's love, respect, and confidential communication. Jesus said to his disciples:

> I no longer call you servants, because a servant does not know his master's business. Instead, I have called you friends, for everything that I learned from my Father I have made known to you.[3]

King David, who knew what that kind of friendship was like, summed it up this way: "The Lord *confides* in those who fear him."[4] Heavenly "gossip." Just between you and God.

---

3 John 15:15.

4 Psalm 25:14 (emphasis added).

Chapter 42

CEO of Heaven and Earth
The Sovereignty of the Son

The sovereignty of Jesus Christ is the best news imaginable!

Now, you may be thinking, *Wait a minute. Isn't it God the Father who is sovereign?*

And you would be right. Except that when it comes to functional sovereignty—in particular, how God's sovereignty applies to *us*—we can't separate the sovereignty of the Father from that of the Son and the Holy Spirit.

Take, for example, what Jesus told his disciples: "All that belongs to the Father is mine."[1] Or his declaration after he had risen from the dead: "All authority in heaven and on earth has been given to me."[2]

Think about that last statement. Any issue that comes up in either the created universe or in the heavenly realm is subject to Jesus's

---

1   John 16:15.

2   Matthew 28:18.

authority. From an earth-based organizational perspective, we would identify that role as President and Chief Executive Officer.

But even that comparison falls short. During the years I spent as a CEO in healthcare, I was always constrained by various laws and regulations, not to mention the mandates of the Board of Directors. Which is a good thing. Earthly power and authority should always be constrained.

By contrast, Jesus, while he works in complete harmony with the Father and the Spirit, "reports" to no one in his role as CEO of heaven and the universe. There is no higher authority.

I suspect many of us aren't used to thinking of Jesus that way. After all, he was born as a baby in Bethlehem, he grew up to be a carpenter and then a rabbi, he preached and healed the sick, and he was cruelly executed while still a young man of about 33. (Of course, it didn't end there!)

It's right that we appreciate his humanity. The incarnation of God through Jesus Christ was what changed everything for us. But we must never let that detract from his sovereign position and role.

Neither should we make the mistake of thinking the Father and the Son differ in their values or their attitude toward us. Here is how author John Mark Comer puts it (in his refreshingly non-religious manner):

> For years, I thought of Yahweh in the Old Testament as parallel with the Father in the New. Like Jesus is a new-comer in the story. That's wrong, and dangerous. It leads to a twisted caricature, as if the Father is the grumpy old warmonger in the Old Testament, and Jesus is the son who went off to Berkeley and came home with all sorts of radical ideas about grace and love and tolerance and basically said, "Come on, Dad, let's not kill everybody. How about I die for them instead?"

This is a gross misreading of the story the Scriptures tell.[3]

Some might find Comer's description offensive, but I would suggest what really is offensive to God is the twisted picture we have of what he's really like.

That happens easily, even to people who spend a lot of time with Jesus. Philip, one of the twelve disciples, once said to Jesus, "Lord, show us the Father and that will be enough for us."

Jesus answered: "Don't you know me, Philip, even after I have been among you such a long time? Anyone who has seen me has seen the Father."[4]

If that weren't clear enough, another Scripture spells it out this way: "The Son is the radiance of God's glory and the exact representation of his being."[5]

And this mind-boggling verse: "For in Christ all the fullness of the Deity lives in bodily form."[6]

Could it be any more straightforward?

Jesus is not a cryptic clue as to the nature of God or a portrait of the kinder, gentler side of God's nature, but *the exact representation of his being*. There is no more precise picture of God the Father than Jesus the Son.

And it's not a watered-down version of Deity that we're getting. (Jesus isn't like 2% milk compared to whole milk.) Instead, in him *all the fullness of the Deity lives in bodily form*.

Not that any of us could fully comprehend the meaning of those statements, but at least we're left with no doubt about who we're dealing with when we're talking about Jesus.

3   John Mark Comer, *God Has a Name* (Grand Rapids: Zondervan, 2017), 58.

4   John 14:8-9.

5   Hebrews 1:3.

6   Colossians 2:9.

While Jesus walked this earth, such claims were commonly seen as blasphemous—which is why he was opposed by the religious leaders and ultimately killed.

It's also why early Christians were sent to their death as they kept insisting that Jesus is Lord, not Caesar.

And it's why even in the 21st century, while extremists persecute and kill Christians, and unbelievers use the name of Jesus as an expression of anger or disgust, the followers of Jesus Christ still honor him as their Lord—the one who died for them but now is seated in the heavenly realms "far above all rule and authority, power and dominion."[7]

Best of all, "far above" doesn't mean far away. Through the Spirit, that ultimate CEO office occupied by Jesus extends from the highest heavens to the humblest of hearts.

---

7   Ephesians 1:20-21.

Chapter 43

What If...?
The Sovereign Foreknowledge of God (Part 1)

Anyone entering politics soon learns how to avoid *gotcha* questions from reporters—"What if *this* happened? What would you do then?"

The safe response? "I'm not going to speculate on hypothetical situations."

It may be a cop-out, but it's a good way of avoiding controversy when someone steps into the public square. And it's generally accepted by the public because, as we'd all agree, nobody knows the future.

In fact, some theologians aren't sure that even *God* knows the future![1]

I believe the Bible teaches that God does know the future and that this truth is a central component of his sovereignty. In fact, he even knows the outcome of hypothetical situations.

---

1   Some, for example, believe God purposely limited his knowledge in order to safeguard humanity's free will.

Let's consider, for example, what Jesus said when he spoke about the towns that had rejected him:

> Woe to you, Chorazin! Woe to you, Bethsaida! For if the miracles that were performed in you had been performed in Tyre and Sidon, they would have repented long ago in sackcloth and ashes.
>
> And you, Capernaum, will you be lifted to the heavens? No, you will go down to Hades. For if the miracles that were performed in you had been performed in Sodom, it would have remained to this day.[2]

It's one thing to believe that prophets in the Bible predicted the future, but this is different. This is Jesus saying he knows how several ancient communities in the Middle East *would have* responded if they had witnessed his miracles. It's a declaration that God's foreknowledge is all encompassing, including not only what *will* happen, but what *would have* happened under different circumstances.[3]

When you think about it, that's an astonishing statement: something only a charlatan or a lunatic—or a sovereign God—would dare to claim.

On one occasion Jesus said to his followers, "Yet there are some of you who do not believe." The apostle John goes on to explain, "For Jesus had known from the beginning which of them did not believe and who would betray him."[4]

The knowledge that some of his followers, including one of the Twelve disciples, did not really believe in him must have been painful for Jesus, but clearly it was a burden he was willing to carry. And, just

---

2   Matthew 11:21, 23.

3   Keep in mind that Jesus said he didn't speak on his own initiative, but only spoke what the Father told him to say (see John 12: 49-50).

4   John 6:64.

as clearly, it did not interfere with his followers' free will—including that of Judas, his betrayer.

On another occasion, when Jesus was prophesying the future destruction of the temple and the signs of the end times, describing scenes of unrelenting hardship and disaster, he added this comforting yet puzzling word: "If those days had not been cut short, no one would survive, but for the sake of the elect those days will be shortened."[5]

In that statement, Jesus reveals supernatural knowledge not only of what *will* happen, but of what God decided to do (shortening the time period) in light of what *would* happen otherwise.

When a person goes through unexpected, life-shaking events, those truths take on a whole new meaning. A few months before my wife's diagnosis of terminal cancer, I had read Matthew 11, the passage about what Jesus said to the unrepentant towns, and journaled the following notes under the heading, "God knows the *What Ifs*":

> *Only Jesus is able to speak about hypothetical situations with complete accuracy and authority.*
>
> *We speculate on what could or would have been—or how someone would have responded in a given situation—but he is able to state such things without any uncertainty or speculation.*
>
> *He knows not only what choices we will make in future, but what choices we* would have made *if certain things had happened. That's the nature of his all-encompassing knowledge— and why we should trust him with everything.*
>
> *He knows every angle, every possible outcome to an infinite degree, because he has no limits.*
>
> *Therefore I can trust God implicitly and completely, without reservation. He knows every detail and every* possible *detail*

5   Matthew 24:22.

or configuration, and he's working all things together for good!
Your sovereignty, God, is the simplest and yet the most complex
truth imaginable.

Those were my thoughts before my world was turned upside
down. They still describe my understanding of God because they're
based on the words of Jesus Christ.

In the first example of Jesus's foreknowledge, when he was speaking about the towns that had rejected him, he dealt with hypothetical scenarios in the *past*. When he referred to followers who didn't
believe, he was dealing with the *present*. And when he prophesied
about the end times, he was talking about the *future*.

Past, present, future, and every possibility—all are equally
exposed to his sovereign view and all are subject (ultimately) to his
sovereign will.

The best "What if?" question we could ever ask ourselves is this:
What if God really is who he says he is?

Chapter 44

Blissfully Unaware
The Sovereign Foreknowledge of God (Part 2)

We're in the third millennium of the Common Era—over 2,000 years since Christ was born—yet millions of otherwise modern, scientifically savvy people still consult their horoscope, just in case the alignment of stars and planets can provide clues for what's ahead.

The desire for knowledge of the future is as strong as ever. Is it just curiosity? An indicator of anxiety? Evidence of control issues? All of the above?

In the time since the unexpected loss of my first wife and my equally unexpected remarriage, I've often thought about our ignorance of the future. How much would I have wanted to know beforehand?

The answer I keep coming back to is *zero*.

Think of it. What would happen if God were to tell us everything about the future? Two personal examples come to mind:

- In the years preceding my wife's death, supposing we were enjoying a nice vacation together somewhere and God said, "I'm going to tell you something about the future. The next time you're here it will be with Dianne, not Margarete." Can you imagine the horrendous burden that knowledge would have placed on my marriage relationship, not to mention my psyche and emotional well-being?

- During the months leading up to Margarete's passing, what if God had told me the exact date of her death? I would have had to cope with the emotional load of knowing all the "last times"—the last time we'd watch a sunset together; the last time we'd share a meal together; the last time we'd share the same bed; the last time we'd share a conversation. For me, that knowledge would have been a curse, robbing us of freedom and normality in our relationship.

Having said all that, God does at times speak about the future. It's called prophecy, and it's given to us as a blessing—or sometimes as a warning.

One of the interesting aspects of prophecies in the Bible is that they are sometimes spoken in the *past tense*, as though God didn't care that they had not yet come to pass—as though everything had already been fulfilled:

- When a priest named Zechariah prophesied following the birth of his son, John the Baptist, he said, "Praise be to the Lord, the God of Israel, / because he has come to his people and redeemed them."[1] This, of course, was before the Redeemer (Jesus) was even born.
- About 700 years earlier when the Assyrians were preparing to attack Jerusalem and godly King Hezekiah prayed for help, the prophet Isaiah sent this message from God against the enemy: "Virgin Daughter Zion /

---

1   Luke 1:68.

despises and mocks you. / Daughter Jerusalem / tosses her head as you flee."[2]

The Assyrians had not yet fled when this prophetic judgment was spoken, so why was it stated as a done deal? The answer is found a few verses later:

Have you not heard?
    Long ago I ordained it.
In days of old I planned it;
    now I have brought it to pass.[3]

It all has to do with the foreknowledge of God and how he pre-ordains certain things.

The reason prophecies can be stated in the past tense is because God is sovereign and his decrees cannot be altered. He doesn't cross his fingers and say, "All things being equal, if everything works out as I'd hoped, and if everyone involved cooperates, this prophetic word should come true (I hope)."

Neither are his decisions based on partial knowledge.

Donald Rumsfeld, defense secretary under former President George W. Bush, was noted (and sometimes vilified) for this statement on the nature of human knowledge:

As we know, there are known knowns; there are things we know we know. We also know there are known unknowns; that is to say we know there are some things we do not know. But there are also unknown unknowns—the ones we don't know we don't know.[4]

---

2   Isaiah 37:22.

3   Isaiah 37:26.

4   https://www.theatlantic.com/politics/archive/2014/03/rumsfelds-knowns-and-unknowns-the-intellectual-history-of-a-quip/359719/.

It's good to recognize the limits of our own knowledge, including those "unknown unknowns," but we should never confuse our restricted knowledge base with the infinite knowledge of Almighty God.

Supernaturally unbounded knowledge is necessary in order for totally dependable direction to be given. If God did not know all possible outcomes—if he too were subject to unknown unknowns—how could he say to us "Do this rather than that"?

I'm so thankful that, as Scripture says, "his understanding has no limit."[5]

I'm also thankful that he understands our limitations in terms of what we can deal with at a certain point in time, that he doesn't overwhelm us with information we're not ready to handle.

That may put me in the category of "blissfully unaware," but that's fine with me. I'm sticking with the best *known known* there is: the reality of a God who knows all, who rules all, and who understands our limitations.

He's the One who graciously shields us from knowledge we cannot bear, while revealing what we do need to know. He mercifully hides certain "dots" from our sight, and uncovers others that were hidden.

Then he helps us learn how it all fits together: how his gracious sovereignty affects us—for this life and the next.

It's understanding reality from a larger perspective; it's seeing by faith.

It's connecting the dots.

---

5   Psalm 147:5.

Appendix

What About the Bible?

The underlying premise of this book is that we can rely on the Bible as the trustworthy and authoritative Word of God. In the following synopsis we look at the basis of that belief and explore some interesting facts and figures surrounding this unique spiritual resource.

The Bible's Unique Role

The Bible is the most popular book in history.[1] Even today, best-seller lists exclude the Bible because it would always be #1, week after week, month after month, year after year.

Here's how a chief religion writer for *Time* magazine once described it:

> Simply put, the Bible is the most influential book of all time…The Bible has done more to shape literature, history, entertainment, and culture than any book ever written. Its

---

1   https://en.wikipedia.org/wiki/Bible.

influence on world history is unparalleled, and shows no signs of abating.[2]

Still, reading the Bible can seem a daunting task. It's lengthy, at times strange, and, depending on your translation, challenging to understand. But billions of people through the ages have found it to be life-giving and transformational.

By the Numbers[3]

- The 66 books of the Bible were written by at least 40 different authors over a period of 1,600 years.
- If printed on normal book paper, a Bible would fill eight volumes.
- About 75% of Bibles sold in America are printed in China, which specializes in printing technology using thin paper.
- Estimates of the number of Bibles printed since 1815 range from five to six billion.
- Currently, over 100 million Bibles are sold or given away each year.
- As of 2019, the complete Bible had been translated into 698 languages; the New Testament into another 1,548; and smaller portions into 1,138 additional languages.[4]
- The YouVersion Bible app had 400 million users worldwide by the end of 2019.

---

2   David Van Biema, "The Case for Teaching the Bible," *Time,* March 22, 2007, http://content.time.com/time/magazine/article/0,9171,1601845,00. html.

3   With statistics readily available online, not all source information will be cited.

4   https://www.wycliffe.org.uk/about/our-impact/.

English Versions of the Bible

- The Bible has been translated from the original Hebrew (Old Testament) and Greek (New Testament) many times over the centuries, reflecting changes in the English language itself, discoveries of ancient manuscripts closer to the time of writing, and different approaches to translation.
- Translation approaches range from "word-for-word" to "thought-for-thought." (Regarding the latter, if you have spent time with people who speak other languages, you will understand the difference between translating the exact words vs communicating the essential meaning.)
- The most popular English translation is the New International Version (NIV), a translation considered roughly midway between word-for-word and thought-for-thought. Next in popularity is the King James Version (KJV), followed by the New Living Translation (NLT).[5]
- If you are not proficient in Old English from Shakespeare's time, you probably will have problems understanding the King James Version (also known as the Authorized Version), which was completed in 1611.

Credibility of the Bible

- The Bible has been the subject of intensive study for the past two millennia, and thousands of books and research articles have been written on it. While there

---

5   https://christianbookexpo.com/bestseller/translations.php?id=0120.

are skeptics among those researchers, there are also tens of thousands of well-grounded and well-educated people who are trained in linguistic, archeological, and theological studies who accept the Bible as the authoritative and completely trustworthy Word of God.

• When atheist Lee Strobel, a hard-nosed investigative reporter (later legal editor) for *The Chicago Tribune*, tried to debunk Christianity in order to convince his wife to give up her faith, he instead came to the conclusion that Jesus was real and the Bible was true.[6] This pattern has been repeated many times by truth-seekers over the years, from the humblest souls to the most distinguished academics.

• One of the most brilliant people I have heard in person is Dr. John Lennox, Emeritus Professor of Mathematics at Oxford and an internationally renowned speaker on the interface of science, philosophy, and religion. (He's earned three doctorate degrees and speaks four languages—which I believe officially qualifies him as a brainiac.) According to Lennox, there should be no conflict between science and faith—including the Bible:

> We study God's revelation both in the natural world and in Scripture with the minds that God has given us. And I believe there is no conflict ultimately between those two sides, properly understood.[7]

---

6   https://leestrobel.com/about. He later wrote his story in the book *The Case for Christ*, which was also the title of the biographical movie released in 2017.

7   *Why and How Should I Read the Bible?* Episode 6, Alpha Film Series (London, UK: Alpha International, 2017), https://www.youtube.com/

"Proper understanding" of course is related to how we *interpret* the Bible. To start with, we need to be aware of the different types of literature contained in its 66 books. Poetry, for example, is often rich in metaphor and imagery, and cannot be handled the same way as didactic teaching. Secondly, we need to recognize that certain words can be used in different ways, which means we don't always have 100% certainty on every point.[8] Thirdly, we need to acknowledge that Bible-believing Christians will disagree on some points of interpretation, even while they agree on the main teaching—the essentials—of the Gospel of Christ.

What the Bible Claims

- Jesus accepted the Scripture (which at that time consisted of the Old Testament) as the inspired and eternal Word of God. When he was tempted by Satan, he didn't use his own authority, but repeatedly said, "It is written…"[9] Here was the Son of God, through whom all things were created, referring to the Scriptures as the final authority. Think of it: The Bible

---

watch?v=ICOeeua-TTQ [Accessed July 20, 2020]. I would heartily recommend this video and the entire Alpha Course.

8   For example, the word "day" in Hebrew has the same variations of meaning as in English: the hours of daylight, a 24-hour day, and an indeterminate period of time (as in "the day of judgment"). That can lead to differing interpretations when it comes to Scriptures like the beginning of Genesis where it refers to the days of creation. Those who believe God used 24-hour days to create are called "young-earth creationists;" those who believe those days represent ages are called "old-earth creationists."

9   Matthew 4:1-11.

is made up of words written down by frail, imperfect men as they were led by the Holy Spirit. If Jesus had such confidence in the Word, shouldn't we?

- But Jesus also put his own words on par with the Old Testament Scriptures, saying, "Heaven and earth will pass away, but my words will never pass away."[10]
- The apostle Paul states, "All Scripture is God-breathed and is useful for teaching, rebuking, correcting and training in righteousness..."[11]
- In his later years, the apostle Peter affirms his role as an eyewitness: "For we did not follow cleverly devised stories when we told you about the coming of our Lord Jesus Christ in power, but we were eyewitnesses of his majesty."[12]
- He also refers to Paul's writings as "Scripture," but acknowledges, "His letters contain some things that are hard to understand..."[13] (something most of us can relate to).
- Jesus claimed that even the Old Testament Scriptures were focused on the coming Christ (himself). Speaking to the religious leaders of the day, he said:

> You study the Scriptures diligently because you think that in them you have eternal life. These are the very Scriptures that testify about me, yet you refuse to come to me to have life.[14]

---

10   Matthew 24:35.

11   2 Timothy 3:16.

12   2 Peter 1:16.

13   2 Peter 3:15-16.

14   John 5:39-40.

- In other words, Bible study is not an end in itself. It's ultimately meant to lead us into a closer relationship with Jesus Christ.

Resources

- Bible websites and apps: Here are some of the most popular sites:
  - BibleGateway.com
  - BibleHub.com
  - Bible.com
  - BibleStudyTools.com
  - YouVersion.com
- Study Bibles: These are Bibles that include commentary, index, notes, maps, charts, and introductions to the books of the Bible.[15]
- Books to help navigate and understand the Bible: One of the best known in this category is *How to Read the Bible for All Its Worth* by Gordon D. Fee & Douglas Stuart.

In Conclusion

While Bible study and research can seem challenging, our regular reading in the Word doesn't need to be complicated, especially as the Holy Spirit helps us understand the practical and personal application of Scripture.

According to the apostle Paul, the Bible was written for our *benefit:*

---

15   When considering a Bible for primary use, it's usually best to choose one where the translation was completed by a team of linguists and Bible scholars rather than one person.

For everything that was written in the past was written
to teach us, so that through the endurance taught in the
Scriptures and the encouragement they provide we might
have hope.[16]

Finally, both Old and New Testament declare God's Word to be
living and enduring—in contrast to human mortality and the rest of
nature. As the apostle Peter quotes the prophet Isaiah:

All people are like grass,
    and all their glory is like the flowers of the field;
the grass withers and the flowers fall,
    but the word of the Lord endures forever.[17]

---

16   Romans 15:4.

17   1 Peter 1:24-25.

Selected Bibliography

Buchanan, Mark. *David: Rise*. Canada: M.A. Buchanan, Inc., 2020.

Comer, John Mark. *God Has a Name*. Grand Rapids, Michigan: Zondervan, 2017.

Fee, Gordon D. and Douglas Stuart. *How to Read the Bible for All Its Worth,* 4th ed. Grand Rapids, Michigan: Zondervan, 2014.

Hall, Dudley. *Grace Works,* updated edition. Euless, TX, 2013.

Keller, Timothy. *Walking with God through Pain and Suffering.* New York: Penguin, 2013.

Lewis, C.S. *The Best of C.S. Lewis.* Washington, DC: Canon Press, 1969.

Lewis, C.S. *The Weight of Glory.* New York: HarperCollins, 2001. First published 1949.

Mason, Mike. *The Gospel According to Job.* Wheaton, Illinois: Crossway, 1994.

Mason, Mike. *Champagne for the Soul.* Vancouver: Regent College Publishing, 2003.

Oliver, David. *All About Heaven.* UK: Malcolm Down Publishing, 2019.

Piper, John. *Future Grace.* Sisters, Oregon: Multnomah Books, 1995.

Rana, Fazale with Hugh Ross. *Who was Adam? A Creation Model Approach to the Origin of Humanity,* 2nd expanded edition. Covina, CA: RTB Press, 2015.

Reimer, Rob. *Soul Care: Seven Transformational Principles for a Healthy Soul.* Franklin, TN: Carpenter's Son Publishing, 2016.

Ross, Hugh. *Beyond the Cosmos: The Transdimensionality of God,* 3rd ed. Covina, CA: RTB Press, 2017.

Ross, Hugh. *The Creator and the Cosmos: How the Latest Scientific Discoveries Reveal God,* 4th ed. Covina, CA: RTB Press, 2018.

Ten Boom, Corrie with John and Elizabeth Sherrill. *The Hiding Place.* New York: Bantam Books, 1971.

Yancey, Philip. *The Question That Never Goes Away.* Grand Rapids, Michigan: Zondervan, 2013.

Acknowledgments

Any attempts to acknowledge the role of other people in our lives are bound to be inadequate. I often recall my dad quoting the apostle Paul, who wrote to the Corinthians, "What do you have that you did not receive?"

That disclaimer aside, I want to express appreciation to a few people in particular:

- My parents and those who were spiritual fathers to me—Bob Birch and Barney Coombs—all of whom now reside in heaven, and my pastor Charlie Whitley, who (I'm happy to say) is still on this earth.
- My late wife Margarete, who wrote before her passing, "All the best with your book. Wish I could have been around to see that dream fulfilled." I don't know how to measure spiritual influence, but it's likely that her generous, faith-filled life impacted me more than any other.
- Writers who inspired me, including Malcolm Muggeridge, Philip Yancey, C.S. Lewis, Mike Mason, John Eldredge, and Mark Buchanan.
- Family and friends who offered ongoing encouragement; Bryn Franklin, whose prophetic

picture influenced my writing approach; and those who graciously provided endorsements.

- Those whose help came in practical ways: the editors and publishing consultants at FriesenPress, and John and Marjorie Wiens, who lent their cabin in the Kootenays to me for "writing weeks."

- My wife Dianne, who is disinclined to take any credit, but whose help has made a huge difference—offering motivation without pressure, reviewing my writing from both a literary and theological standpoint, and serving as a valuable sounding board throughout.

- My Lord and Savior, Jesus Christ, who, with the Father and the Holy Spirit, gives meaning and hope to all of life and eternity.

I will always be grateful.
Arthur

About the Author

Although writing has been a long-term goal, Arthur Enns spent the first few decades in other careers: radio—including CHQM and QM-FM in Vancouver, where he hosted the all-night jazz show before assuming the role of Music Director; pastor of Vernon Christian Fellowship, a twelve-year period that included hosting a weekly TV show on behalf of the Vernon Ministerial Association and being elected as a Trustee and Board Chair of Vernon Jubilee Hospital; and healthcare administration, serving as CEO of Menno Place in Abbotsford and Board Chair of the Denominational Healthcare Association of British Columbia.

Arthur considers marriage, family, and church relationships to be an unparalleled blessing in his life, and has dedicated this book to the memory of his late wife Margarete, whose faith and encouragement provided a strong impetus to his writing career.

These days, time away from the computer (and an office crammed with books, papers, sticky notes, and jazz CDs) is spent visiting children and grandchildren, traveling with his wife Dianne, and hiking the trails overlooking the lakes of British Columbia's Okanagan Valley.

Lightning Source UK Ltd.
Milton Keynes UK
UKHW040639271022
411161UK00008B/124/J